In His Steps Today

Marti Hefley

HANNIBAL BOOKS
www.hannibalbooks.com

Printed in the United States of America
by Lightning Source
Cover design by Cyndi Allison
Library of Congress Control 75-42375
ISBN 978-1-934749-93-7
All Scripture taken from the King James Version
of the Holy Bible. Used by permission.

Hannibal Books
P.O. Box 461592
Garland, Texas 75046
1-800-747-0738
www.hannibalbooks.com

(To order more copies of *In His Steps Today* mail a check for
$14.95 plus $4 shipping, with 50 cents extra for each additional
book, to Hannibal Books at the address above.)

Dedication

To my siblings—
Charlene, Laura, Shirley, Faith, and Sammy

Chapter 1

We <u>would</u> have to have snow, Heather Novak thought irritably. *Now Don will be even later getting home. Every time I need him, he seems to have a last-minute customer. Naturally a sale is more important than I am.*

She continued arranging her freshly baked brownies on the doily-topped silver platter and nibbled on any crumbs that happened to fall. When two tempting morsels refused to fit into her fancy pattern, she solved the problem by eating them.

If this snow keeps up, no one will be here tonight. I'll have to live with these brownies in the house all day tomorrow. If I don't stop picking at no-no's, I won't be able to squeeze into this pantsuit again, she scolded herself as she pulled down the tunic top of the snug, cranberry-red outfit.

Heather carried the tray across the wide, slate-floored entry hall and into the family room she had decorated so lovingly. Four thickly carpeted blue steps led down into the huge, paneled room. A natural rock fireplace flanked by floor-to-ceiling bookcases dominated the wall facing her. To the left was a wall of glass doors that led to the terrace beyond. Two oversized leather couches faced each other on either side of the glass-topped table in front of the fireplace. Everything was in place; all was shining and perfect.

As she centered the tray on the glass table, Heather glided to the open-weave, burlap drapes and pushed the button that pulled them back. The outside lighting revealed a white fairyland. *At least the snow looks beautiful*, she conceded. *And per-*

haps Wanda will be afraid to drive in it alone. It certainly wouldn't hurt my feelings in the least if our femme fatale *didn't join us tonight.*

Heather enjoyed the rest of "The Group", as they called themselves. They had started with a few couples from their church and had met every other Thursday night. That was a little more than a year ago. Since then, others had joined in; some had dropped out, but The Group remained Heather's principal social outlet. Group members followed a prescribed Scripture-reading program, with discussion usually beginning about something they had read since the previous get-together. This soon developed into making practical applications to their daily lives. For the most part the members of The Group were open and frank with each other, although they sometimes had some very animated disagreements.

"Hi, honey, I'm home!" Don called from the front door. As he pulled off his overcoat and boots, Heather returned to the hall for a perfunctory kiss. "What's to eat?" he asked briskly.

"Ham and au gratin potatoes I served half an hour ago. I hope it's still edible. Pull up a stool to the serving bar; you can eat in the kitchen." She took his plate from the oven and set it on the placemat she had laid out for him.

"You only have 10 minutes before they'll start arriving. I'd like to have your dishes put away before anyone sees my messy kitchen," she explained while she poured him a tall glass of milk.

Don watched his wife's retreating figure as she returned the milk to the fridge. Her waddle made him realize how much time had lapsed since his college sweetheart had won beauty-queen honors.

"Are the boys asleep?" he asked as he changed his line of thought.

"They're in bed. I doubt if they're asleep yet, though. I

gave them baths before dinner so I could clean up after them. You know what a mess that pair of 9-year-olds can make."

"Heather, you are too uptight about having this house on display all the time," Don muttered. "I'll bet you've been washing plant leaves with milk again just to make them shinier. That's all you've thought about for the two years we've lived here!" he accused her.

"And all you think about is selling cars!" she countered.

"If I didn't sell cars, you wouldn't have this house!" he retorted. "And you couldn't make a full-time career of decorating it."

The doorbell chimed. A look of panic crossed Heather's face.

"Oh, calm down, honey," Don said, relenting. "You answer the door and take our guests directly to the family room so they don't see my dirty dishes. I'll stick these in the dishwasher when I'm through."

She flashed him a big smile and displayed her dimples. As she walked toward the door, she ran her fingers through her dark-brown hair.

"I'll be in as soon as I tell the boys good night and tuck them in again," he called as he gulped down the last of his milk.

Heather opened the door to a blast of frigid wind and swirling snow. Towering Kenny Campbell leaped in and shut the door against the cold. "At times like this I think I should return to the Southland for the winter," he drawled.

Kenny was the all-pro shortstop for the Chicago White Sox and, like the Novaks, lived in a far-western suburb. As the tallest player ever to play shortstop in the majors, local sportswriters had dubbed him "the tall stop". His Will Rogers-style folksiness had made him a favorite with the fans; Heather enjoyed his delightful sense of humor.

"Where's Sally Ann?" Heather asked as she took the heavy, fleece-lined coat from her shivering guest.

"Oh, Mary Alice has the sniffles; Sally Ann didn't want to leave her," Kenny explained. "Even though she doesn't want to admit it, Sally Ann isn't exactly running over with energy these days either."

"With another baby due in a couple of months, I can understand that. Three babies in three years is quite an accomplishment. I'm glad I had twins."

"Where are those rascals anyway?" Kenny asked. "Do I have time to say *hi* to them?"

"They would love it, Kenny, but please don't. You are nice to offer, but when you play with them, they get so excited that they would never get to sleep. Why don't you light the fire for me instead?"

"Yes, ma'am. Be glad to. A fireplace is one household appliance this ole country boy knows how to work." Grinning, he knelt down, pulled open the fire screen, and craned his neck to see if the flue was open.

Heather couldn't help but smile. At times he was so awkward that he barely seemed to be the same guy who played ball so gracefully.

"Heather, this is weird," he said with a puzzled look. "I don't see a speck of soot in this fireplace. Did you wax in there or something?"

"Hardly," Heather laughed. "But I did clean it out today."

"Well, if I tell folks back home about this, they'll think I'm exaggerating again," he declared as he shook his head.

The bell sounded again; Heather hurried back to the door. As she admitted Jan and Al Bonnell, she noticed a golden Mustang pull into their long, circular driveway, a feature typical of the four-acre estates in plush Inverness.

"Hey, why the frown?" the diminutive Jan chirped. "A fine

welcome!"

"I'm sorry," Heather replied as she consciously put on a smile. "It—it's just the weather. Hate to see everyone having to buck the blowing drifts. Did you have any problems?"

"Well, it's really coming down, but the plows are keeping the main roads pretty clear," Al replied while he unwound the six-foot-long scarf that Jan had knit him for their first Christmas together. "The secondary roads are clogging up though; I doubt if we'll have much of a crowd tonight."

Heather glanced out to see Wanda Hendricks scurrying up the walk as she pulled her beige coat tightly about her. The furry collar framed her face; her thick, golden hair served as the only covering to her head. With her cheeks flushed with the cold, she bounded up the steps. As Wanda entered the warmth of the hallway, Heather noticed how the snowflakes on her long lashes accented her large green eyes.

She's absolutely gorgeous, Heather thought. *I can't stand her.*

Al gallantly took Wanda's coat. "Good evening, everyone," Wanda purred in her soft alto voice. "This storm makes me feel right at home," she said. Her comment referred to her native Minnesota.

"But aren't your legs freezing?" Jan asked pointedly. "I can't imagine wearing a skirt on a night like this. Pants are so much more practical."

"I'm used to skirts," Wanda explained. "Besides, I really don't have the legs for pants."

Al looked at her long, willowy torso and opened his mouth to comment but thought better of it and said nothing.

"I was wondering whether you'd even get out on a night like this," Heather ventured.

"I debated it a while," Wanda admitted. "But I didn't have to drive far. I so seldom leave the grounds, I believed I really

9

needed to get away. I never seem to get out from under my work."

"*Hmmmm,* I can see why that would be important," Al agreed as they walked toward the family room. "Especially when working with retarded adults. You need to get your mind off them occasionally. Have you ever considered moving?"

"Yes, but my cottage is rent-free; that compensates for a rather low salary. The only rental property near here is out of my price range."

They entered the inviting room to find Kenny standing before a roaring fire; he had a look of satisfaction on his face. "Now y'all know my real talent," he drawled.

Wanda sat down on the black slate hearth to enjoy the warmth. "That's a talent not to be demeaned on such a cold night," she said softly with a toss of her blonde mane. "Especially if you have a car heater that isn't working."

Don had entered just in time to hear her comment and the sympathetic response of the group. "Tell you what, Wanda," he said. "You take my car home tonight. I'll drive yours to work and get the boys in the repair department to fix it tomorrow. I can drop it by on the way home."

"Oh, I couldn't put you to all that trouble," Wanda protested.

"No problem," Don insisted. "After all, I sold you that car. I feel a moral obligation to keep it running smoothly," he continued. He sounded like the glib salesman he was.

"Wow, I've never heard of a car dealer who gives that kind of service," Al teased. "Do all your customers get that kind of treatment?"

"Of course," Don smirked with mock sincerity. "I want to keep my franchise."

I'll bet, Heather thought as she fumed inwardly. She looked indignantly at the only single member of The Group.

Wanda was stroking the big calico cat, Bonnie, who had curled up in her lap. The cat purred contentedly as Wanda ran her fingers through the animal's silky hair.

She's even got my cat charmed, Heather thought jealously. *Now that I think of it, Wanda rather resembles a cat with her slanted eyes and that soft angora sweater.*

"How's your project at work?" Don asked Al, who was reputed to be the resident boy genius at International Scientific Computers.

"Oh, don't get him started!" wailed Jan. "Wouldn't you rather hear about things down at the public library?" Everyone laughed understandingly. Al had an overwhelming enthusiasm for "his" computer and would always gladly relate in great detail and at great length its latest accomplishments. He often lost his lay audience after the first few sentences.

"*Huh!*" Al snorted. "The most interesting thing about that antiquated library is that the building hasn't collapsed yet. Someday computers are going to make libraries obsolete anyway."

The musical sound of the doorbell interrupted the discussion.

"Well, another brave soul has arrived," Kenny quipped.

"Maybe it's just a stranded stranger seeking refuge," Al suggested.

Don rose to answer the door as Heather started serving hot coffee from the urn behind the bar. "Maybe this will help thaw everyone out," she said.

Don returned with Josh and Jackie Pittman in tow. Dr. Joshua Pittman, the pediatric resident at nearby Holy Name Hospital and his beautiful wife, Jackie, a nurse, were the only black members of The Group and the only black residents of Arlington, an adjoining suburb of some 50,000 people.

"I'm so glad you could be here," Heather said so warmly

that Jackie impulsively gave her a quick hug.

"I always enjoy being here," she responded. After others welcomed her, Jackie collapsed into a huge beanbag chair. "We sure picked us some night to show up, didn't we?" she said animatedly as she snuggled into the bag.

"We couldn't make it last time and didn't want to miss twice in a row," her more dignified husband explained as he took a cup of coffee from his hostess.

The brownies were passed; Heather was pleased that everyone seemed to enjoy them. She noticed that Wanda took one polite bite, then put her brownie on the hearth and promptly forgot about it. Heather declined to take one. She said, "I really don't need any" and placed the plate near Al, where she was certain the rest would disappear.

"Have we missed anything?" Josh asked. He typically got right to the matter at hand.

"No," Kenny replied. "We've been kinda waiting, in case the snow made anyone late. I doubt if anyone else is going to get here," he prophesied with a glance out the glass doors at the growing white mounds. "I'll have to admit that I'm rather glad there are only a few of us tonight, because I have something I'd like to discuss, if it's agreeable with the rest of you." He paused; then, encouraged by nods of agreement, he continued.

"The other day at the drugstore I bought a paperback book that has really started me thinking. I'd never read anything like it." He leaned forward and placed bony elbows on his knees, with his hands clasped tightly together. "Perhaps I'd better explain why it has affected me so," he said hesitantly and cleared his throat. "I didn't really encourage Sally Ann to be here tonight, because I haven't told her about this. I'd appreciate none of you mentioning it to her yet." As he glanced around the circle, each pair of eyes pledged silence.

"Nothing official has been said, but I've heard substantial rumors that I might be traded."

A feeling of disbelief swept through The Group.

"Why on earth would they do that?" Don asked incredulously. "You're the best shortstop they've ever had!"

"Well, the word is that they're trying to swap me for a sensational young pitcher on the West Coast. You gotta remember that a baseball player is over the hill at 30. They've begun counting down my playing days. Also, a new ruling says that after 10 years with the same team, they can't sell a player without his permission. That was passed for the players' protection, but it makes a team a little hesitant to keep you that long."

"And how long have you been with the club?" Wanda asked.

"Eight years," he replied significantly. "Now, don't forget, nothing is official about this. That's why I don't want to upset Sally Ann when nothing might happen. But it's a weird feeling realizing that you don't 'own' yourself.

"Anyway, that might be why this book got to me so much. It's all about people who decide to really follow the Lord in every phase of their lives—to make decisions that I'm not free to make. Maybe nobody is free in this day and time. That's why I'd like to know what y'all think.

"I've only been a Christian a year. I have been trying to live the way I thought a Christian should. I give my testimony whenever I get the chance and speak at churches and for banquets and stuff, but this idea of making decisions as Jesus would is new to me."

"Just what book did you discover?" Heather asked in anticipation.

Kenny pulled a pint-sized paperback from the hip pocket of his jeans and slid it across the glass table toward her. The bright red letters of the title were clear for all to see: *In His Steps.**

---

*Charles M. Sheldon, *In His Steps* (Chicago: Moody Press, 1956).

Chapter 2

"Oh, yeah, everyone's read that," Al responded a bit condescendingly. The rest agreed, except Josh Pittman, who picked up the book and began leafing through it.

"It's new to me, too, Kenny," he confided.

"That's because it's not a medical book," Jackie said a bit critically.

"And when did you read it?" Josh asked his wife.

"Oh, *In His Steps* is required reading for all preachers' kids," she quipped. "It's about a minister who challenges people in his congregation to vow to always ask themselves what Jesus would do before they make any decision in their lives. Those who make the pledge band together and report their experiences.

"It's been years since I read it, so I've forgotten a lot of the details. As I recall, I thought it very old-fashioned."

"Yes," Al agreed, "the moralistic values were quite simplistic. The decisions were all so obvious; either the people chose the good or the bad. But real-life decisions are so often between the good and the better."

"Is the book based on fact?" Josh asked. "Did a real group of people make such an all-consuming commitment?"

No one knew the answer.

"The back cover gives a little information," Kenny volunteered. "It says millions of copies of the book have been sold in most major languages. It's the all-time Christian bestseller."

"But does it tell anything about the author and where he got his idea?" Jan asked.

"No, but I'd be interested in knowing that; wouldn't you?" Kenny asked.

"I could look him up at the library. At the next meeting I could share any information I find," Jan volunteered.

"Good," declared Kenny. "Maybe that could help me. I just wonder whether the challenge for the characters in that book could still be applied in our lives today."

"I see your problem, Kenny," Don mused. "In our complex world we don't always easily know what Jesus would do in some situations."

"Exactly. And this bothers me. How could I declare that for the rest of my life I'll always decide just as Jesus would? I don't even own myself! I can't even decide where I'll play next year or whether I'll play."

"But is it just professional sports that hem people in?" Heather asked. "We all face certain limitations."

"That's for sure," Don agreed. "I own my business, but I'm tied down by rules and regulations. I must maintain certain standards to keep my franchise—labor laws, the Better Business Bureau, city codes and restrictions, plus Ralph Nader!

"And that's not even mentioning the fact that I have to please my customers, or I'll go out of business. I have to keep so many records it's almost strangulation in triplicate."

"It's getting to be like that in medicine, too," Josh sighed. "That's one reason I prefer being a resident in a teaching hospital rather than going into private practice. I'd make more money being in my own practice, but I'd have all the hassle of bureaucratic restrictions."

"Is anyone really free anymore?" Kenny asked. "Are we all so bound down by the system that we haven't the freedom to mold our lives the way we choose?"

"Well, I have real decision-making power at ISC," Al declared importantly. "When an edict comes down from above, I have the prerogative of accepting it," he paused for effect, "or quitting."

They all laughed understandingly.

"That about says it," Jan conceded. "Maybe that's why I want to be a writer. As a freelancer, I could make my own schedule choose as I wanted to."

"Yeah," interrupted Al. "Do your own thing; keep getting those pink slips in the mail. Writers have to conform too, or they don't sell. What did that editor tell you?"

"Oh, that."

"Is he referring to the continuing-education article?" Heather asked.

"Yes. You see, I've been working on an article I entitled 'Your Library Card: The Key to a Continuing Education'," Jan explained to the others. "Heather and I have discussed the project at great length. She gave me some good ideas. At least I thought they were good. As Al so sweetly mentioned, it was rejected. But I didn't get another pink slip! I got a personal letter from the editor suggesting some revisions, so it can't be that bad of a job. I'll make a sale yet!"

"Of course you will," Jackie encouraged her. "Anyone with your intelligence and determination can do it."

"I don't know," Kenny pondered. "I think you have a lot of nerve to try. When I go out to speak, I sort of have a captive audience. They have to sit there and listen to my stories about growing up way back in the hills and about big-league baseball. By the time I get to sharing my faith, they're listenin' from force of habit. But putting your thoughts on paper for some expert up in an office somewhere to look over and criticize each word—to me that seems like a tough proposition."

"Sure it is," Al agreed. "I'm proud of Jan for what she has done and will do. But the point I'm making is that a writer is hemmed in, too. The person has to write *what* the editors want and the *way* they want it."

"I see." Kenny nodded. "In this book, *In His Steps,* a newspaperman owned a paper so he could run things the way he wanted."

"And today things just aren't that easy—not for many people anyway," Don added. "Too often today the business owns the person instead of the person owning the business. Becoming enslaved is so easy."

"What do you think, Wanda?" Jackie asked as she tried to draw out the silent member of the group.

"Well, it's been so long since I read the book, I really don't believe I can criticize it. You've gotten my curiosity up though, Kenny. I'm going to re-read it this week."

"That's a good suggestion," Jackie responded. "On the way home we can pick up a copy at the drugstore. Then you can read it too, Josh."

Josh had been skimming through the book, but now he returned it to Kenny. "I don't know," he said cryptically. "I really don't see how I could identify with any of those characters. They all seem to be WASPs with a double W—Wealthy White Anglo-Saxon Protestants."

A burdened silence fell on the group. A half-burned log slipped in the fireplace; it sent up sparks that caused the calico cat to jump from Wanda's lap and skitter from the room. Don cleared his throat but said nothing.

"I can see where that might be a problem," Kenny finally drawled. "Those Yankees in the book didn't much remind me of my hillbilly rearin' either."

Josh laughed at the homespun philosophy. "I get your point, Kenny," he admitted.

"And he's right," Jackie defended him. "Just because we're different from those characters doesn't mean we can't respond to the challenges they faced. But we'd each have to respond in our own way, according to our own circumstances. It's kind of tough to think of Jesus as a black, female nurse. Yet, if I were to accept the challenge, that's what I'd have to do. I'd have to think, what would Jesus do if He were me? How would He react to my life situations?"

"Wow, that's far out!" Jan gasped. "What would Jesus do as a female in today's society?"

"I don't understand why, but for some reason I have trouble seeing Jesus as a car salesperson," Don quipped. That got a laugh.

"You know, it would be an interesting experiment, though," Al mused. "Jesus as a computer expert!"

"Or a would-be writer-librarian," Jan added.

"Jesus at bat!" Kenny announced.

"This really does sound exciting!" Jackie exclaimed. "Even more challenging than in the 'good ole days.'"

"Yeah! Let's try it!" Al enthused.

"Wait a minute," Wanda interrupted softly. "A decision like that shouldn't be taken lightly. You're talking about a lifetime commitment to something that might be very difficult."

"Wanda's right," Al agreed. "I tend to get carried away with my enthusiasm. If we made a pact like that, it would have to be a solemn, well-thought-out, rational decision."

"And no one should be pressured into it just because the rest of us are for it," Jan added.

"But how can we make such a commitment when we don't even know if keeping it is possible?" Kenny asked. "We're right back to where I started."

"But would we have to make it a lifelong thing?" Heather asked.

"That's it!" Al responded as he caught her idea. "We could try it for a week. I mean, how many earth-shaking decisions would we have to make this week?"

"And if we find it doesn't work, we'll have no punishment or guilt feelings. We'll want everyone to feel free to share how they coped with the situations that arose, whether or not they felt they really reacted as Jesus would."

"Now we're getting somewhere," Kenny replied. "We could try it for just one week to see if this is possible."

"With no public announcements before the church, as in the book," Al stated. "We'll keep it to ourselves, for this week anyway, until we see how it works."

"I don't think we should have to keep it a secret," Jan disagreed. "I mean, someone might ask us why we are doing something different than usual. We shouldn't be ashamed to admit that we're trying to live as Jesus would."

"Oh, yeah, sure," Al conceded. "I just mean we don't have to run a public notice in the *Tribune* or anything."

"I'll agree to try it for a week," Josh declared.

The decision was unanimous. "And Sally Ann will go along with us too," Kenny added confidently.

"How can you make a decision like that for another person?" Jan demanded a bit too vehemently.

"Oh, well, I only mean, I'm sure she would want to."

"Watch it, Jan," Al suggested, with a look that indicated they had discussed this previously.

"Oh, I'm sorry, Kenny. It's not my prerogative to say how you should treat your wife. Maybe in your culture it's accepted that a wife is merely an extension of her husband. But it seems to me that a decision of this sort has to be a personal thing."

"Now don't go women's lib on me, Jan," Kenny drawled. "I said that because Sally Ann read the book this week, too. I believe she'll want to join us. I wouldn't try to force her."

"OK, now let's set up some guidelines for this experiment," Al suggested authoritatively. "We will each make decision as we, as individuals, think Jesus would make in our lives. But we will make them as ourselves, according to the personalities God has given us."

"And using the principles taught in the New Testament," Jackie added.

"Agreed," Al continued. "But we must remember that these decisions are personal things; we can't try to impose on one another's freedom of choice. What is right for one person in a given situation might not work for another. We have to feel free to share our experiences with one another, or we'll lose the value of the group experiment."

"Right," Don declared. "And we can meet here next week and discuss what has happened and how we coped with it. Since it's not the regular Thursday for The Group, we could meet here again and not mix up the system. That's OK with you, isn't it, Heather?"

Heather gave a rather weak smile and reluctantly nodded agreement.

"Well, that should certainly be an interesting get-together," Josh declared as he glanced at his watch. "If we are going to stop and pick up a book on the way home, we'll have to hurry," he told Jackie.

"Yeah, I guess so," his gregarious wife sighed. "I hate to be the one to break up the party, but I'll bow to your logic," she muttered with an impish grin.

"I think we had all better be logical, or we might be snowed in," Al declared with a nod toward the patio doors where the swirling snow was continuing to mount.

"I need to get home early anyway," Kenny declared. He unfolded from the couch and stretched his long limbs. "I have speaking engagements for the next three nights, so I'd like to get home before my wife goes to sleep."

"You know, I never have heard you speak, Kenny. I'll bet you do a good job," Heather commented as she began stacking cups and saucers.

"Well, I'll be telling my tall tales at a little storefront church in the inner city on Sunday night. I'm sure the folks there would be glad to have you along."

"Don?" Heather asked with a quizzical look.

"Sure thing. Tell you what, Kenny, we have to come right near your house to get on the tollway anyway. Why don't we pick you up? We can go in together."

"Great. See you about 6 or 6:15."

As everyone started toward the hall, Don held out his hand to Wanda. "Give me your keys, young lady. I'll get your Mustang out of the way and warm up my LTD for you."

"Oh, you really don't have to take my car in for me, Don," Wanda protested with a shake of her thick tresses. "I can attend to it."

"I insist," Don commanded. "Let's have those keys."

Wanda obediently dropped her keys into Don's hand. He rewarded her with a big smile. With growing irritation Heather observed the little scene.

After the guests had bundled up and scurried out into the downy night, Heather carried the dirty dishes into the kitchen. She lined them up in the dishwasher, poured soap powder into the little plastic container, slammed the door shut, and pushed the lock with vehemence. She poked the *on* button; the sucking noise of the machine began.

Don still hadn't returned to the inside, so Heather mounted the stairs to the bedroom alone. She crossed the 30 feet of the room to the windows that overlooked the front drive. Glancing through the sheer curtains, she saw Don and Wanda standing by the car talking. The car door was open; it threw a soft light onto the pair. Although the sound of their laughter could not be heard through the storm glass windows, clearly Don and Wanda were enjoying some private joke.

Well, Lord Jesus, what shall I decide about that? Heather thought rebelliously.

Chapter 3

Friday morning began routinely for the Novaks. Heather awakened her identical cherubs from deep slumber by calling, "Wake-up time, boys. Come on. You'll have to hurry to beat Daddy to breakfast. He's already shaving."

The twins bounded out of bed; they didn't want to miss a precious minute of the time they got to spend with Don each morning. As usual, they managed to beat him to the kitchen by a few seconds.

At the breakfast table Don read a few Bible verses, as Heather served the scrambled eggs and bacon, hot biscuits and honey, and orange juice. As she sat down, they joined hands for prayer.

After the meal the boys bundled up while Heather lined up their books, lunches, skates, and hockey sticks. "I don't see how you're going to fit all this stuff in Wanda's little car," she complained irritably.

"Oh, it'll be fun, Mom," Timmy squealed.

"Yeah, that's a neat lil' car," Tommy agreed.

"That's the spirit, men," Don grinned at them. "We'll be real pioneers braving the cold as our forefathers did before us." He gave Heather a parting smack, opened the front door, and called, "Let's go, troops!"

Heather shut the door on their noisy confusion as she closed herself in the quiet, empty house. *That was some kiss,* she said as she began cleaning up the breakfast mess. *He gets up early to drive the twins to school when they could just as easily take the bus. He goes to as many of their hockey games as he possibly can and always devotes Sunday afternoons to them, but when does he make time just for me? He just takes me for granted*, she sighed.

All right, Heather, she told herself, *it's getting too much when you start being jealous of your own sons.*

But I'm not really jealous of them, she argued with her inner ego. *I just want him to make me feel special, too, the way he used to. Why, if he'd just give me one of those big smiles like he gave Wanda last night, I'd still melt. Instead, he stands out in the cold flirting with her; then he wonders why I don't feel romantic when he finally gets inside.*

He says he loves me. Maybe I just need more self-confidence. She began praying, "Lord Jesus, how do I get more confidence? Then maybe I'd feel more willing to enter into the discussions of The Group. I have ideas that are good, but I keep them to myself. I'll bet everyone thinks the one-week trial period was Al's idea, when actually I thought of it first. He just took over.

"Of course, it doesn't really matter who gets the credit, does it? Jan sometimes takes my suggestions and uses them in her articles, but I'd never do anything constructive with my ideas, so she might as well. Besides, she can put them into words so much better than I.

"I'm afraid I'm a little envious of Jan, Lord. Forgive me? It's just that I wish I had more of her confidence. She seems so young and full of life and determined. If I were more like that, maybe Don would be more proud of me. I wouldn't be so suspicious every time he smiles at another woman.

Maybe the shiny, newlywed love that Jan and Al have will dull with time, too, Heather thought. *Does love have to lose its luster? I can't help but wonder if their days begin as monotonously as mine do.*

Jan was drying her hair with the electric blower as she regarded her reflection in the dressing-room mirror. She approved of her large brown eyes but wished her nose wasn't quite so long. Her waist-length, straight brown hair which had never been cut pleased her, too, but she wished it could be as thick and healthy-looking as Wanda's was.

Al walked by and patted her bottom, nuzzled her neck, and admonished, "You'd better move it, Little Bit, or we'll miss the 7:55."

Jan bristled at the nickname; she held the firm conviction that people tended to treat her like a child just because she was short. The thought galled her. She switched off the blow-dryer, set it down, and whirled around.

"Would you take me more seriously if I were half a foot taller?" she demanded.

"No way," Al replied as he put his arms around her. "I like you just the way you are. You're my doll baby." She wiggled loose and stalked to the bureau to pull out a pair of warm socks.

"Honey, I can't help the fact that you look 15," Al pleaded. "I know you're 21 and very mature. Give yourself time. Before you know it, you're going to be worrying about old age creeping up on you."

Al brushed his hair a few strokes and then walked into the living room to pick out a book to read on the train. He wondered what Jesus would choose; surely He wouldn't read the Bible all the time. He finally decided he and Jesus needed to make a trip to the bookstore. In the meantime he reread one of C. S. Lewis's science fiction books.

"You about ready?" he called. "I don't know how enthusiastic our old Chevy's going to be about starting this morning."

Jan stuffed her lunch and manuscript into her oversized tote bag so that while she was on the train, she could work on the education article and then join Al in the dash from their apartment to the car. The snow had stopped falling, but the wind was now whipping it into a blizzard effect.

"Hope this thing starts," Al said fervently as he scraped snow off the windshield. The duo jumped in and listened apprehensively to the discouraging sound of the grinding of the motor.

"Oh, come on, baby, start just one more time," Al pleaded. "Man, for the rent we pay, we certainly should have a garage," he complained for the umpteenth time.

"Moving out here was your decision," Jan reminded him.

"And you weren't exactly pulled screaming and kicking into this lap of luxury," Al countered. He tried pumping the accelerator.

"You're going to flood it again," Jan warned.

Just then the motor caught, sputtered, and roared into action. Al shot a self-satisfied grin in Jan's direction and smugly announced, "Looks as if we'll make it after all."

The drifting snow slowed the traffic, so they arrived at the station with only a couple of minutes to spare. As they shivered onto the platform, waiting, Jan turned her back to the wind and stomped her feet in an effort to keep warm.

Al looked down at his diminutive bride and smiled. He reached down and turned up her collar to frame her face and keep the wind off the back of her neck. In the process he gave her cheek a soft pat.

Jan's huge brown eyes reflected the warmth of her responding glance. As the train roared into the station, Al mouthed the words, "I love you." For a brief, special moment they were all alone amid the sea of surging people.

As the crowd pushed them aboard, they paused to check for the *no-smoking* sign and then entered the car to the left. Jan took a window seat and pulled out her manuscript as Al plopped beside her when the train lurched forward.

"You going to work on that same article?" Al asked.

"Well, I can't give up on it when the editor of *Woman's World* says it 'shows promise.'"

"I never knew anyone could be so proud of a rejection," Al teased.

"Not just a rejection. When you get a personal letter from the managing editor, it means it got past a number of readers. Editors don't bother to write letters about just any manuscript. It must have some merit; besides, Heather likes it. I value her opinion."

"What makes her an expert?"

"I didn't say she was an expert, but she does read a lot and is a very intelligent woman. She's frank enough to tell me if she doesn't like something. If it's too long or not clear or just boring, she will say so. You always tell me everything is 'real good', so I don't know if it is or not."

"Guess I am a little prejudiced," he admitted as he opened his book and slouched down to a more comfortable position.

With her red marking pen in hand Jan turned back to her manuscript. Until the train pulled into the darkness of the terminal, she marked out a word here and there and wrote little notes to herself in the margins.

By this time Heather had finished making beds and straightening the bathroom and was pouring herself a second cup of coffee. She carried it toward the living room, where an inspection from the threshold revealed the picture-book perfection she had arranged the day before in anticipation of her guests. Glancing across the hall at the formal dining room, she decided nothing needed to be done in either room, so she walked down the hall to the more-comfortable family room and sat on the top step. It offered a view of the whole room.

As she sipped her scalding beverage, the thought dawned on her, *Invite Wanda for lunch.*

Humph! She laughed at herself. *That would be something. Wanda here for lunch. And driving up in Don's car, no less.*

Let's see, Don should be at work by now, she thought as she glanced at her watch and quickly figured the time involved in dropping the boys off at school, backtracking, and then taking the 45-minute drive to work. *Of course, with the snow he might be delayed. I wonder if he will face any great decisions today. At least he'll have more to do than sit and wait for some dust to fall. Think I'll call him.*

At least I don't have to be concerned about Alice any more, she thought while she punched out Don's phone number. His charming young secretary, who recently had acquired a sparkly solitaire engagement ring, answered with a cheery "Good morning, Novak Ford."

"Good morning, Alice," Heather responded. "Has Don made it in yet?"

"Yes," Alice replied hesitantly, "but I don't think this would be a good time to talk to him."

"Anything wrong?"

"No, I don't think so. The new salesman, Hal, made a sale early this morning, which is really unusual, especially since Don is ordinarily the first one in. Anyway, when I handed him the contract, instead of being pleased, he scowled and went dashing out to the showroom to look for Hal.

"Maybe he filled out the forms wrong or something, I don't know. Would you like me to tell him to call you later?"

"I'd appreciate that, Alice. Thank you very much."

Alice smiled as she hung up the receiver. Heather's attitude toward the Alice had changed so obviously since the secretary had announced her engagement. Alice found this really amusing, although she had to admit she still had a slight crush on her boss of five years. But that seemed natural, for they spent a lot of time together; Don was a good-looking guy. Perhaps what intrigued her most was his seemingly contradictory personality. He had all the charm of a natural con man, yet he was scrupulously honest.

Don and Hal passed by Alice without even noticing her and entered Don's spacious office.

"I'm impressed with you clinching a deal so early in the morning," Don said as he dropped into his oversized swivel chair. "Most of the salesmen weren't even here at that time."

"Aw, just beginners' luck," the newcomer replied, but the pride showing on his face belied his words. "This little old couple had decided they wanted a new car before they left for Florida tomorrow. They knew what they wanted; we had it in stock, so it wasn't difficult to get them to sign on the dotted line. I made quite a deal, didn't I?"

"You certainly did, Hal. I'm a little curious about it. What kind of condition was their trade-in in?"

"Oh, nothing wrong with it that a good tune-up and a little spray of 'eau de new car' wouldn't fix," Hal said. He grinned confidently as he sat down on the corner of Don's big desk.

"But they paid full retail price. You gave them $100 less for their old car than the Blue Book suggests."

"But . . . but," Hal sputtered. "They drove away as pleased as could be. They certainly weren't unhappy about the deal. You said when you hired me that you wanted happy customers; that's what they are."

"Perhaps so," Don murmured. He pursed his lips in contemplation. He rocked back and forth in his chair a few times and then continued, "I just don't feel right about it. Just because they didn't realize they could save some cash by dickering a little bit, I wouldn't have taken advantage of them like that."

"Are you trying to tell me that I made too good a deal? That you're worried about making too much profit?" the pudgy salesman demanded.

"Yes. Yes, that's what I'm saying," Don replied absently. His mind was not on the salesman's questions but on a far more soul-searching one. He sat up straight, pulled his chair under the massive desk, and dropped both fists on the desk top. Decisively Don said, "We're going to return a hundred dollars to them."

Hal's mouth dropped in amazement, but Don raised his hand to assure him, "You won't lose any commission—this time. I'll make up the difference. But in the future let's try to give even the most naive customer a square deal.

"I want you to write them a covering letter explaining that a mistake was made. Alice will type it up for you and make out the check. We'll make up the difference in goodwill. Next time they buy a car, you can depend on it; they'll come to us."

"The next time!" Hal snorted. "That car will outlast the two of them. They're already over the hill."

"Maybe so," Don replied determinedly, "but I want that letter written. Immediately!"

Muttering under his breath, Hal stormed out of the office. "That guy's got to be nuts!" a bewildered Alice overheard him say as he cut through her office.

"You have a complaint on line three," Alice said through the intercom, "and Heather wants you to call."

Don talked to the irate customer, who believed the repair department had replaced some parts in his car unnecessarily. Don managed to smooth the ruffled feathers and believed the firm would continue to get the man's business, but he made a mental note to check things out with the service manager soon.

"Anything wrong?" Heather asked when Don returned her call.

"No, but something happened that has gotten me to thinking. You know I've always tried to treat my customers fairly. Even when I was selling shoes as I worked my way through school, I always tried to make friends with potential buyers. I like the warm feeling I get when people have confidence in me. I really try not to take advantage of that confidence.

"But what about my employees, Heather? Am I responsible for the actions of my salespeople? And I just got a disturbing report about the service department."

"What are you going to do?" Heather asked.

"I'm not sure, but that new salesman, Hal, pulled a real gyp on an unsuspecting couple this morning. I just couldn't let it pass. Jesus clearly would never allow such a thing.

"But now I'm wondering whether I'm responsible for holding a tighter reign on all my employees. Policing them might have some serious repercussions, moneywise. And I could lose some valuable people. Hal was really aggravated."

"Well, the only possible way you could devote yourself more completely to your business would be to buy a bed and move in down there," Heather replied. She was displeased at the peevish whine she realized was in her voice.

"I know," Don agreed, "I have responsibilities to my family, too. I struggle to know how to arrange priorities sometimes. Perhaps that's the greatest challenge in this experiment about deciding as Jesus would.

"Maybe my immigrant parents ingrained the Protestant work ethic in me too strongly. Or that could be just a cop-out. I don't know, but I tell you what; if you can wait dinner until 7, I'll try my best to be home to eat with you and the boys."

"Oh, they'll wait gladly," Heather assured him. "And afterward we could make popcorn in the fireplace and play games with them or something—just to be together."

"Now I can't promise, but I'll certainly do my best. If an

emergency should arise, I'll call."

"Oh, you can do it if you try; I know you can. It'll be fun. See you then!" She signed off gleefully. Her whole day was suddenly brighter.

We'll eat in the dining room, she decided. *I'll set the table fancy and make stroganoff. And for dessert? German chocolate cake; that will please him. It's been a long time since I made one from scratch.*

And after the boys are tucked safely in bed, I might just put on the new negligee he gave me for Christmas and waltz back down and shock him, she thought. She grinned mischievously.

Most of her afternoon was devoted to preparing the elaborate meal. When the boys arrived home from school, she fed them a snack to hold them over until 7 but very self-righteously denied herself any extra food.

Despite her cheerful mood, the boys were particularly quarrelsome that afternoon. The sun had appeared about noon; the snow had turned to slush. That forced the twins indoors. They picked and fussed and fought with each other until in desperation she sat them down for a "conference."

"Now hear this," she began with mock sternness, "Daddy is making a special effort to get home early tonight just to be with us. I realize that dinner is later than usual and you are hungry, but you can hold out a little while longer. He'll be here soon; if we want him to do this more often, we'll all have to try to make this a pleasant evening."

They agreed to try, but by 7:15 Timmy pleaded, "Couldn't we just have something while we're waiting?"

"He'll be here any minute, I'm sure. He promised he'd call if anything held him up," Heather protested. "Eating together will really be nice."

But by 7:30 she gave in and fed the twins. At 8 she began picking at the food herself—"tasting" from the stove and "testing" to see if it was still good.

By 8:30 she was stuffed and angry. She stalked to the phone and began punching the buttons vehemently. Then a thought struck her. *Wanda.* Don was supposed to take their friend's car back to her on the way home. *If I call the office and they say he left two hours ago, I'll feel like a fool. What could I say?* she asked herself as she slowly returned the receiver to its wall socket.

At 9 she shooed the boys off to bed without the daily bath she always insisted on. She got ready for bed herself and then sat in the overstuffed chair near her bedroom window, where she could see the driveway.

She tried finishing a novel she had been reading but found concentrating to be difficult. "If an accident had happened, I would have been notified by now," she finally decided. "And if he's been at work all this time, he wouldn't stop by and change cars with Wanda. It's too late to go by and disturb anyone."

She stood up, pulled back the panels of the sheer under-curtains, and peered into the darkness. She hoped to see the little Mustang turn into the driveway. To her great relief, the twin beams of a car started toward the house. Then the automatic garage door swung open and the lights flashed on as they revealed the LTD.

Infuriated, she threw her book across the room, turned out the light, and jumped into bed. As she pretended to be asleep, she seethed with a variety of conflicting emotions.

Chapter 4

Saturday morning traditionally was Heather's day to sleep late. Don would sneak out to make his own breakfast. When the boys woke, they got themselves some cereal and watched cartoons until she arose.

This morning Don deliberately shoved his drawers shut with a bang, rattled the closet door unnecessarily, and sat on the bed to put on his shoes and socks. Heather was quite aware that he was trying to wake her so they could talk, but she continued to feign sleep.

Why talk? she thought. *Get things out in the open? That wouldn't help. Besides, I'd rather not know the details. I'll just continue to be a dutiful housewife and mother and pretend that everything's fine. But I can't talk about it. Not now.*

She felt the peculiar, warm sensation that meant he was looking at her and trying to decide whether she was really sleeping. Then he left the room. Soon she heard him driving off without taking time for breakfast.

She drifted off into a troubled sleep that was interrupted by the ringing of the phone. Automatically her hand reached for the bedside instrument. She shook her tousled head as she tried to clear away the sleep.

"Hello."

"Heather, this is Jan. I've got something I have to share with you," the younger woman chirped excitedly. "Say, were you asleep? I'm sorry, I didn't realize—"

"Oh, that's all right. I need to get up anyway. This sudden

35

January thaw has messed up the ice. I'm going to have to drive the boys all the way to Northbrook to the indoor rink for their game today. But you've gotten me curious. What's happened?"

"Well, first, I want you to realize I wouldn't tell this to just anyone, but I think you'll understand. You see, at the library I sit and process books for hours sometimes. I become totally unaware of what I am doing. It's so automatic—so completely nothing—that I can do it with no conscious thought at all. The only thing good about it is I can think about my writing and check out books at the same time.

"Well, yesterday I happened to look up and notice this quaint little old lady who is one of our regulars. She always wears a kooky-looking hat with a bird on it. She visits the library a couple times a week anyway and checks out romantic or historical novels.

"Well, when I glanced at her, I noticed the wind had ruffled the feathers of that ridiculous bird; I must have smiled. And Heather, this really gets me! She reached out and grabbed my hand. Tears welled up behind her bifocals. She said, 'Bless you, dearie. That's the first smile anyone has given me in weeks.'

"I—I just didn't know what to say. I hadn't even really smiled at her; yet, that sweet, lonely old lady was so thrilled at what she felt was a warm, human response. I processed her books. She hurried away with a big smile and a cheery good-bye."

"Oh, that was nice, Jan," Heather commented. "You'll have to keep an eye out for her from now on. Maybe you could get to be her friend. Sounds as if she could use one."

"Oh, I'll watch out for her all right, but she really got me to thinking. I encounter so many people at work, but I don't even take the time to smile. I'm so wrapped up in my own thoughts most of the time that I have no time for people. I just

36

know Jesus wouldn't be like that!

"Why, I couldn't even share the incident with anyone at the library. I don't have a single friend there. Isn't that a disgrace? I always spend my breaks doing research. I bring my lunch and eat while I read information about some article.

"I guess I got in that habit while I was working my way through school and had to study in spare moments, but now I realize that's the problem with my writing, too. I'm so involved with books and facts and statistics that I forget about people. I just don't relate with my readers. And that's what the editor was trying to tell me. I need reader identification."

"Wait a minute, Jan," Heather pleaded. "You're losing me. What's the connection between the little old lady and the editor?"

"Because she made me realize I need to identify with people, not impress them. Everything I've written has been impressive, but impressing the reader, or the editor, isn't what's important. It doesn't matter that I graduated *magna cum laude* or that I made Who's Who in American Colleges. What is important is meeting the needs of my readers. And that's what Jesus would do. He wouldn't be a superintelligent writer talking down to some lowly homemaker type and telling her she needed to start learning something.

"Well, I stayed up to 1 o'clock this morning rewriting it. And it's good now, Heather; I know it is. It's stimulating. I really believe it will challenge the reader and encourage her to continue her education."

"Well, that's great, Jan. I'm really happy for you. Would you like to have me read it?"

"Oh, I'll bring a copy to church tomorrow if you'd like, but I'm mailing it in today. I think the reason I kept wanting you to read my stuff was I knew deep down that something was lacking, but I couldn't put my finger on it."

"Well, I'm glad you discovered it," Heather said sincerely. "And thanks a lot for sharing it with me."

"Sure thing. See you tomorrow. Bye."

"Bye," Heather responded softly. *So she doesn't need my opinion anymore,* she thought wistfully. *Well, Lord, what people am I supposed to relate to?* A glance at the clock reminded her that the twins still depended on her. The rest of her day would be devoted to them.

When Don dragged in late that evening, the boys were already taking their baths.

"Boy, this has been one long day," he complained as he collapsed into his chair.

"I'll serve your meal immediately," Heather announced coldly.

"Oh, Heather, don't tell me you are still playing the martyr. If you would just listen, I can explain—"

"I'm sorry, but I must get the boys out of the tub," she explained as she placed his food in front of him. She poured his milk and then walked briskly from the room.

When she was tucking the boys in, she bent over to kiss Tommy good night, but he turned away from her. He exclaimed, "Aw, Mom, you treat us like babies. We're getting too old for all that mush."

She retreated from the room quickly before they could see the tears she could no longer control. She had never felt more alone.

At breakfast the next morning the boys were their usual rowdy selves. If they had noticed their parents were unusually quiet or that their father had spent the night in the guest room, they didn't mention it. Only one minor skirmish occurred— over which twin sat by which window in the car; then they were off to Sunday school.

Heather entered the new children's education building eagerly. When the twins were that age, she had begun teaching 4-year-olds in the beginner department. When the boys were promoted, she had stayed on and had taught the class ever since. This age group delighted and challenged her. She found them capable of learning much more than was usually expected. She took special pleasure in astounding parents by the accomplishments of her pupils.

"Hello, Miz Noback," a curly haired blond youngster sang as she entered the classroom. He ran toward her at full speed with both arms extended. She bent down and scooped him up. "I missed you!" he announced. He hugged her so tightly, she nearly lost her balance.

"And I missed you too, Billy," she replied. "I heard that you had the mumps."

"Yes," he agreed. He nodded his head as she set him down. "I looked like this," he said as he puffed out his cheeks in chipmunk fashion.

Heather managed to chuckle despite the stinging behind her eyes. *At least little kids love me*, she thought as she stooped to sit on the low stool Don had made for her years before. She keeping the youngsters' attention easier when she was down at their eye level. As the children gathered around, she got out the hand puppets she used to tell stories.

"I don't know how you do it!" one of the mothers exclaimed when she arrived to pick up her daughter after class. "Leaving Suzy at Sunday school was always traumatic. She would cry and stomp her feet and fuss, but now she loves being here. You have really won her over."

"She's a real charmer," Heather proclaimed. "I enjoy having her. I love this class; we have a lot of fun together." With a much lighter step Heather made her way to the vestibule of the church.

As she walked down the aisle toward their usual pew, she noticed Wanda hand Don a single key, smile, and then retreat to the other side of the building. *Not in church!* she thought with her heart pounding in her throat. *How could they?* Instead of sitting in the space Don had left for her, she squeezed past him and the two boys and sat at the far side of the pew. The sermon was totally incomprehensible to her.

Later, at the dinner table, Don asked, "Well, Heather, are you ready to talk to me now?"

"I really don't believe a discussion is in order in front of the children," she answered, as she continued to place tasteless food in her mouth.

"Well, I'm not going to beg you," he snapped disgustedly. He threw down his napkin and stomped away from the table.

After she cleared away the dishes, Heather took two headache tablets and lay down in hopes that the throbbing in her head would disappear. As she slid off into slumber, she was vaguely aware of Don and the boys going down to the workshop to finish some project they had started together.

"Heather. Heather," Don called softly while gently shaking her. "Come on, sleepyhead. I'm going to get the babysitter. You need to fix us a sandwich or something. We'll have to hurry, or Kenny will be waiting."

"What? Kenny? Oh, I'd forgotten all about going to hear him speak tonight. Do we have to?"

"It's kind of late to back out now. Besides, I called Karen; she's expecting me to pick her up any minute."

"Oh, all right. I had no idea I'd take such a long nap. I haven't slept very well the last couple of nights."

"Neither have I," he replied poignantly.

"Glad to see ya," Kenny exclaimed. He opened the front car door and put a long leg inside. This forced Heather to slide over next to Don. "It's a long ride into town alone."

"Sally Ann isn't going?" Heather asked disappointedly.

"Naw, we have trouble getting baby-sitters for our little ones, especially when we have to leave this early. Getting a 1-year-old and a 2-year-old ready for bed at the same time is quite a job. If they are already asleep for the night, we can get a teen-ager to sit; otherwise it's tough."

"That's too bad. I was looking forward to being with her."

"You're going to have to give me directions, Kenny," Don reminded him.

"Sure thing. Just get on the tollway. I'll warn you when we get to our exit. This is the first time I've spoken at this church, but I think I can find it. Matter of fact, I do most of my speaking at church banquets or civic-club lunches, but I haven't taken any out-of-town engagements for the rest of the off-season because of Sally Ann's condition."

"How are things going with the experiment?" Don asked.

"Well, I can't say I've faced any crisis so far this week," Kenny drawled. "I was already committed to these three speaking engagements; I clearly believed that Jesus would have honored these commitments. But I've been doing a lot of thinking.

"It was something Jan said the other night—about the way a man should treat his wife. I mean, Jesus wouldn't have a wife, so we don't have a real example. I'll have to admit that back in the hills a man kind of considers his wife as a sort of prize possession, kind of like a good coon dog!"

"*Humph!*" Heather snorted indignantly.

"I knew you'd like that!" Kenny laughed. "But I have been doing some serious thinking. Sally Ann has never really had a life of her own. I robbed the cradle, I guess you might say— married her right out of high school. And I'm the one who was eager to have a large family right away. That is the way they do back home; I waited a long time to marry, so I guess I wanted to make up for lost time.

"But then, since I've been a Christian, I've been away from home more and more and left Sally Ann with all the responsibility. That doesn't seem right, but I'm just trying to serve the Lord. What do you think, Don? How would Jesus treat a wife?"

Heather held her breath as she strained to hear Don's mumbled response.

"That's a difficult proposition, Kenny. It's tough to know. To a certain extent it would depend on the circumstances. I believe, though, that the ideal situation would be a shared relationship. Not just sharing a home or bed, but sharing your whole life; if you could serve the Lord together, that would be really great."

"Yeah," Kenny agreed wistfully. "Oh, our exit is just ahead. We'll be heading north."

The early darkness of winter had already fallen by the time they were nearing their destination, but it wasn't dark enough to hide the seedy rows of dilapidated apartment buildings. Heather stared; she was appalled at abandoned cars rusting in the streets, overflowing garbage containers, discarded furniture, and just plain junk scattered around.

"I—I've never seen this part of town," she ventured as she noticed tattered plastic curtains showing through dingy windows.

"This neighborhood is called 'Little Appalachia' by the newspapers," Kenny explained. "It's considered a hillbilly haven since so many people from the South live here."

"I think I would rather starve on an old dirt farm than move to this."

"Many of these folks were literally doing just that before they became desperate enough to move to the big city to find work. They've seen some mighty tough times, but that doesn't mean they have lost their faith or determination or pride. Most of them are still doing the best they can.

"I met this pastor, J.D. Gleary, at a banquet he and his wife, Marilyn, attended not long ago. They can tell some sad stories, but they keep plugging away trying to help these people.

"Watch the numbers now, Don. We should almost be there. There it is, up ahead—with the light out front."

Heather felt a little apprehensive as they parked in front of a building that had at one time been a small store of some kind. The bottom half of the two glass walls had been painted; the upper half was so dirty she could hardly see through.

"Better lock up," Kenny suggested.

As they entered the building, Kenny was greeted warmly by a young man who evidently was the pastor. After quick introductions, J.D. excused himself. "I'll see if I can get you seats," he whispered.

As the pastor stopped to talk to two young men seated on the aisle in about the middle of the long room, Heather glanced about. All the folding chairs seemed to be filled. A few young men stood against the dingy wall at one side of the building, two rows of benches held some giggling youngsters at the front, and some work-worn men squatted down near the upright piano.

The two boys the pastor with whom the pastor had talked got up and shuffled toward the back as he motioned for the Novaks to take their seats.

"Thank you," Heather whispered as the two youths passed them. All she got in return was a belligerent stare. As she sat in the vacated chair, she smiled at the grey-haired, middle-aged woman next to her. Wary eyes watched as Don helped her out of her coat; then her eyes turned coldly to the front.

The unexpected rebuff made Heather feel very out of place. She glanced around, but no one else seemed to want to be friendly either. *What have I gotten myself into?* she wondered as the inept pianist began plunking away at the out-of-tune, tinny-sounding instrument.

The congregation rose and began slowly, so slowly, singing "Rock of Ages." Heather noticed the leathery neck of the frail man standing in front of her and the gnarled fingers of the woman sharing his songbook. They had three young children with them, so they couldn't be very old, yet they seemed very tired. Burdened.

A strange sensation clutched Heather. She felt herself no longer sitting in the middle of the group but rather viewing the whole scene from a distance. She saw beyond the threadbare clothes and care-lined faces to the longing in their eyes as their voices throbbed emotionally to "Let me hide myself in Thee", as the song said.

She felt a strong desire to hold these people—to comfort and love them. "O Lord," she prayed, "these people have so many needs, yet they seem to have such great faith in You. I can hear it in their singing. I've never really thought about what an easy life I've had—still have. I've had so many blessings—so many opportunities, but I've taken them so much for granted. I even—I'm so ashamed—I even spend so much of my time feeling sorry for myself. How can you forgive me?"

Chapter 5

After the pastor introduced him, Kenny unfolded himself from his chair and stood behind the homemade pulpit.

"I hope you folks don't take offense," he began, "but I feel like a bear in a cage back there. I think I'll just come around front and join the crowd.

"Now, Pastor Gleary has already mentioned about every honor I've ever won in baseball, so I won't have to bore you with any more statistics. Instead, I'd like to tell you a little about myself. I hail from so far back in the hills that we used to look up the chimney to see if the cows were coming home."

An understanding ripple of laughter rolled through the crowd. Heather noticed the husband and wife in front of her look at each other and grin. She imagined they must have heard that tale before.

"I recall one time when this country cousin of mine, name of Billy Buck, and I got lost in a cave. We were about 12 or 13 at the time. Now, we were supposed to be off fishing, but they weren't biting. We got bored and began explorin'. We'd both been warned many times about goin' into that particular cave, but we didn't see where it would hurt to take just a little look-see.

"We rigged us up a kind of a torch with an ole horse muzzle full of pine knots that we tied on the end of a green sycamore pole. In we went. Well, you know it was so nice and cool in there out of the hot sun. It seemed to be a nice, clean cave with high ceilings and rock floor that we felt quite brave about exploring further and further. Then, before we realized what was happening, the muzzle slid off the pole, our pine knots scattered and died out. We were left in the dark."

The people in the audience seemed to hold their breaths. Men and women alike leaned forward in rapt attention. Even the children had stopped squirming and were listening intently.

"Well, we weren't much worried," Kenny continued. "We didn't think we'd gone too far, so we started groping our way back to the entrance. I never will understand it though, but that ol' opening just disappeared. We wandered around quite a while before we could admit to ourselves that we were lost. Then when we finally did 'fess up, we got to arguing about what to do about it.

"Billy Buck wanted to follow the downhill slope. He figured that was the broader, easier way to go. But I was scared of falling into a hole without a bottom down there where the cave got bigger and deeper, so I insisted we try working our way up. Well, we finally decided to try it my way.

"I never will know how many hours we wandered around in that cave, but it couldn't have been half as long as it seemed. After a long while our stomachs started growling; we were both a wishin' we weren't quite so big, so's we could cry.

"Well, when we had about decided our plight was hopeless, I spotted a little pinpoint of light way up ahead. I let out a whoop; the two of us started off like a couple of coon dogs after a fresh scent. The cave got narrower and lower. We had to get down on our hands and knees and crawl; then we just squirmed and wiggled. Good thing we were both such skinny kids, or we never would have made it out of that little ole rabbit hole.

"But, man, was I ever glad to get out in the sunshine! I never felt anything so good! The world looked so beautiful.

We were way over on the other side of the mountain from where we had started. We took some time to get our bearings and head for home, but we knew we were out. We were shouting happy!

"Now my trusting in Christ was a lot like that experience. I had been warned about sin, but that didn't stop me from trying my own way. And I wandered around in the darkness for a long time before I realized I was lost. Then I didn't know the way out. I spent a long time groping and looking for a way out of my predicament.

"But, you know, when I saw the light, I knew that was the way. I found it to be a straight, narrow path, but how good it was to warm my old heart in the sunshine of God's love. I've only been a Christian a year now. Sometimes I have the feeling I've lost my bearings; I don't know for sure which way I should take next. But I know I'm free. I know I'm a headin' home."

Kenny turned and smiled at the pastor, who rose and announced a hymn number. After the closing prayer, the people swarmed around Kenny; they asked him questions and thanked him for being there. The Novaks observed the warm response he was receiving, but no corresponding welcome was offered them. They encountered no feeling of hostility; the people just seemed to ignore them.

After the crowd had thinned out, J.D. went to Kenny and slapped him on the back. "That was great," he declared. "Just great. They really responded to you. This was the biggest attendance we have ever had—even beat last Easter morning—and they were here because of you. Not just because you are a big-name ballplayer, but because you are their kind of people. I think you were a real source of encouragement to them."

"Well, thank you kindly, J.D. I enjoyed being here."

"Look, we live right across the street. Why don't you and your friends walk over and have a cup of coffee with Marilyn and me? I'd like to discuss some of the problems these folks face. Many of them have a tough time adjusting to city life, but they just don't have any jobs back home."

"Yeah, I know what you mean," Kenny responded. "And thank you for the invitation, but it's an hour's drive home. I don't like leaving Sally Ann alone too long," he explained as he started toward the door. "She hasn't been feeling too well. Didn't even make it to church this morning," the Novaks heard him say as they took Kenny's hint and exited into the clear, cold night.

They climbed into the car. Don started the motor to warm the heater while they waited for Kenny to finish saying good-bye. Just as he seemed ready to leave, the pastor's wife walked up. The conversation started all over again. He finally managed to talk himself over to the car door, gave one last wave, and jumped in.

"Sorry to keep you waiting," he apologized.

"Oh, that's perfectly all right," Heather responded. "If you want, we could stay for coffee. I mean, they seem so thrilled to have you here; don't feel you have to rush away because of us."

"Oh, I really do want to get back to Sally Ann. Besides, I need time to think before I make any commitments, which is what they are getting at."

"Well, tonight was really special, Kenny," Heather volunteered. "When we first went in there, I thought those were the coldest, most unfriendly people I had ever been with. But when you started talking, I could feel them warming up as they responded to you. It was really beautiful. I'm so glad I decided to go tonight."

"Yeah, this was special all right," Kenny agreed. "Special

and unusual. This was entirely different from most of my speaking engagements."

"In what way?" Don asked.

"Well, I usually speak to well-fed, contented people still finishing up their desserts and drinking coffee. They like to hear lots of baseball stories. The back-home kind of stuff is just thrown in for laughs.

"As a matter of fact, even the laughter is different. These folks were laughing with me, not at me. Their response was just—well, different. I can't quite explain it."

"Identification," Heather volunteered softly.

"What?" Kenny asked.

"Identification," she repeated. "It's something Jan was telling me about yesterday. She says that before you can really help people, you have to identify with them."

Hmmmm, Kenny muttered thoughtfully. "Yeah, I see her point. Mountain people tend to be suspicious of outsiders; I'm afraid that's why you found them unfriendly, Heather. I hope they didn't hurt your feelings. But, see, you go in there dressed so nice, with your hair fixed fancy and looking like a million bucks. How could they possibly identify with you? You seem like an alien being to them. Ah, no offense?"

"Of course not. I understand, but I feel sad. I'd like to help these people if I could, but would they accept an outsider?"

"Well, do-gooders often turn them off. I don't have that excuse though. Last fall I was offered a job coaching some basketball teams in this area. The teams are sponsored by some of the civic clubs. I turned it down because of the commitments I had made to speak at various places."

"That's a shame," Don commented. "I'll bet you could strike up a real rapport with these kids."

"Yeah, I guess I could." Kenny sighed. "But at the time, well, the front office encourages us to speak during the off-season. They even set up some engagements for us. It gets the team's name in the local papers and keeps fans thinking of baseball during the winter months.

"I've just made what seemed the obvious decision at the time. I never stopped to think what Jesus would decide in that situation. But if Jesus were living my life," he drawled thoughtfully, "He certainly could identify more with these people than with the ones I've been entertaining.

"Hey, *entertaining*," he declared with a snap of his fingers. "That's just the word—*entertaining*. All this time I've been going around entertaining people but not really getting involved with them. Usually after I speak, I sign a lot of autographs and get told how great I am. It's—What do you call it?—an ego trip? No one asked for my autograph tonight, but I really believe I accomplished more than merely entertaining folks.

"Too bad Sally Ann didn't get to go with us tonight. This is something she could get involved with, too. Marilyn said something tonight about sewing classes and things she holds for the women. By the time next season is over, the baby will be old enough that maybe Sally Ann and I could work together helping our own kind of folks.

"Sure wish I could figure something for Tuesday—"

"Oh, Kenny, that sounds like an exciting possibility. Just the perfect way for you to serve the Lord together. But what about Tuesday?"

"Oh, the Glearys invited us to dinner. It would give Sally Ann an opportunity to get to know them and some of the projects they have going. Certainly would help us in deciding just how we could help best. But that brings us right back to the babysitting problem. We'd never find anyone that early; to bundle the kids up and take them along would be such a job that I know Sally Ann would rather just stay home. Besides, its kinda tough to talk with a couple of toddlers demanding attention."

"Well, I have the perfect solution to that," Heather commented.

"Oh?" asked Kenny. "What?"

"Me."

"You? Oh, Heather, I didn't mean that. I wasn't hinting, really," Kenny protested in embarrassment.

"I'm sure you weren't." She smiled. "But how many times did you take the boys to a ball game last summer? I owe you the favor. And I haven't anything else to do."

"But they're really a handful."

"Hey, you're talking to the mother of twins, remember? I'll manage fine. I'll just bring the boys with me; we'll all have dinner at your house with your babies. Don doesn't get home 'til late anyway, so it's all settled."

"I certainly do appreciate the offer, Heather, but I don't know if Sally Ann will want to impose like that."

"Kenny," Heather insisted, "you tell your self-reliant, independent wife that I felt compelled to volunteer because that is what I believed Jesus would do in my circumstances."

"Well, if you put it that way, we just can't refuse, can we? I certainly do appreciate it, Heather," he declared as Don pulled into his driveway. "I'll have Sally Ann call you to set up the time," he said as he opened the door and climbed out. "It's a real blessing just to know you folks," he declared. He left to share his experience with his wife.

Heather slouched down in the corner Kenny had just vacated. The empty space between her and Don filled with a cold silence as she retreated to her own thoughts.

Well, Lord, she thought, *I can't write like Jan. She doesn't even seem to need my opinions anymore. Her article is good; I could think of no improvements. And Kenny was clear that he didn't believe I would be accepted if I tried to help those dislo-cated hill people. But I can babysit. I guess that's all I'm good for.*

Chapter 6

On Mondays Heather traditionally scheduled a thorough housecleaning. She vacuumed or mopped all the floors, dusted all furniture, polished all mirrors and shiny objects, and scrubbed the tubs and sinks. Then she felt free to devote part of the rest of the week working on whatever decorating project she had lined up.

But this morning she felt discouraged. Perhaps this was because she had run out of projects. Last week she had papered the walls of the laundry room and painted the shelves to match. What else could she do? She wished spring were here so she could work in the yard.

After she finished with the breakfast chores and fed the cat, she poured herself another cup of coffee and sat down on one of the leather-topped stools at the breakfast bar for a good "think".

Maybe I can talk myself into enough enthusiasm to get going, she thought. *Perhaps my problem is not having any decorating projects lined up, but I like everything the way I have it. Why redo something just for the sake of redoing it?*

I wish Don would call. I've kept up this iceberg routine about as long as I can take it. I think I'm punishing myself more than I am him. Of course, I could call him. But, no. It's his place to make the overtures.

INVITE WANDA TO LUNCH. Now why did I think of that again? No way can I picture myself having a cozy little get-together with her. Maybe my subconscious would like to get the whole affair out into the open. If so, I'm overruling it. I—

All right. Come on now, Heather, she scolded herself. You're supposed to be talking yourself into getting busy. After all, you have this beautiful house; now it's your responsibility to take care of it.

I wonder how many of those people at the little church last night have ever even seen the inside of a house as nice as this one. I'll bet those women wouldn't complain about having nothing to do but caring for such a home.

Besides, it's my own choice. I could get a job or go back to school or anything I wanted, but I love this house. Maybe my problem is I love it too much and devote too much time and attention to it. Can a person have a love affair with an inanimate object? Jan teases Al about his computer being his mistress. I'll bet Al would understand how I feel about my house.

At that moment Jan and Al had just reached the towering glass-and-steel International Scientific Computers Building. They blew each other a kiss; Jan continued down the street toward the library. For a few seconds Al watched her plaid-coated figure until it was swallowed up by a crowd of taller strangers.

He pushed his way through the glass revolving doors and decided to stop by the main computer floor before he went to his office. He hoped the customer engineers had finished installing the new disks.

Exiting from the elevator to the eighth floor, he turned to his right and marched briskly toward the glass wall barricade which kept unauthorized personnel from entering. Shoving his key card into the slot to the right of the door, he triggered the mechanism which caused it to slide open. The closed-circuit television camera followed him as he walked up the rubberized ramp that led to the raised computer floor. At the top of the ramp, another camera turned on him and, after it had recognized him, slid the next glass door open.

The familiar hum of the computers seemed like a musical background to the quiet activity in the huge, florescent-lighted room. The cool, sterile, smoke-free environment had been specifically created for the protection of the delicate computer system. A half-dozen operators were working at their terminals scattered at random among the large, canary yellow boxes which housed various components of the complex ISC-4000 computer.

He walked across the huge room and dodged the square holes in the floor where suction tools had lifted sections of tile to provide access to the web of cables beneath. He approached one of the largest yellow boxes where teams of engineers had been working around the clock to install the 16 new disks. If everything had gone smoothly, chances were they might possibly have finished it over the weekend.

"How's it going?" he asked the three engineers who were standing back admiring their handiwork with pleased expressions on their faces.

"Fine, Al," replied a good-looking young black man in blue overalls. "I think your toy is ready for you to start playing with. We've removed the probes to monitor it. Everything is working all right."

"Great. We'll try it out." Al walked over to the nearest terminal and told the operator, "Carol, we're ready to feed them. Start the programs to begin initializing and using the new disks. Shift half of your data input to them and back up to take in case of possible failure. If you have any problems, let me know."

"Sure thing, Al."

After some good-natured bantering with the engineers, Al gave the computer an affectionate pat and walked over to the secure elevator which would take him to his office on the floor above. Besides his total absorption in computer technology, Al enjoyed the informal congeniality within the industry. His work was so stimulating that he found the fact amusing that he was paid for doing it.

Entering his office, he was annoyed to find a note he had left himself as a reminder of a luncheon appointment. He usually became so absorbed in his projects that he worked right through the lunch hour.

He turned on his desk-side terminal and informed the computer of his arrival. It replied by listing which of his subordinates had signed in and what they were doing. Al decided that, since his day was going to be broken up, he would spend the morning testing out the new disks himself. He informed the computer of his plans; it typed out, "OK."

Al was gratified to find everything running smoothly, for the disks represented another small step forward in the international project of storing all available scientific information in one computer system. With the 214 million characters of information each disk could hold, Al figured they would be about 1/10,000th done with the task. If they could continue to feed information faster than new knowledge became available, the project might be completed in another 200 years. He had no worries about job security.

His concentration was so complete that before he realized it, noon had arrived. He stretched his arms and twisted his head around to relieve the kinks, then donned his hat and coat and left his office.

"Oh!" his secretary exclaimed when she saw him. She had a look of consternation on her face. "Mr. Kline's office called and said the meeting had been postponed. I figured I wouldn't interrupt you but just let you work on through. You never remember appointments if I don't call you!"

"Oh, well, I wrote myself a note this time. Don't worry about it. Now that I've stopped, I guess I might as well go eat."

When he stepped out of the building into the throng of busy pedestrians, he found the sun had made a rare winter appearance. The air was so invigorating that he decided to walk the six blocks to his favorite Italian restaurant, Mamma Mia's. The exercise would do him good.

As Al strolled along, he took out a piece of chewing gum, rolled it into a little ball, and popped it into his mouth. He carelessly dropped the paper on the sidewalk. Continuing along, a thought in capital letters dawned on him: *WOULD JESUS LITTER?*

Al blinked in surprise. *Worrying about dropping a little piece of paper was going a little too far,* he decided as he hurried down the street. *But would He?* the thought persisted. He slowed his pace, shook his head, and decided he didn't want to become fanatical about this thing. Al always had been a bit of a literalist though. If he said he was going to do a thing, he did it determinedly. He couldn't let it pass. The thought might seem silly, but he knew Jesus wouldn't pollute the earth in even such a small way.

Resolutely Al swung on his heel and started back. His eyes darted left and right as he searched for the wrapper. He hoped wouldn't spot it. But there it was, blown against a building. Feeling rather sheepish about anyone observing his actions, he stopped and leaned against the wall as if he were waiting for someone. When he believed no one would notice, he bent down, picked up the offending scrap, and stuffed it in his overcoat pocket.

Sighing in relief, he turned and started back toward the restaurant, but his path was barred by a seedy-looking young man wearing what appeared to be an authentic World War II surplus jacket. The youth had a bundle of cheaply printed newspapers under his arm. Pushing one into Al's face, he snarled, "Buy a paper, buddy? The inside story of what life is really like. We tell it like it is."

"Yeah, I've read your rag," Al admitted. "Your editors could use a few grammar lessons, among other things."

"Aw, come on. It's only a buck."

"At that price someone is making a tremendous profit. Who gets it all?"

"I do," was the frank reply. Something about the honesty of the answer and the grin that accompanied it appealed to Al. He laughed and reached into his pocket.

"Oh, I can't," Al remembered suddenly.

"What do you mean you can't? Don't tell me you can't afford it?"

"Well, no, that's not it. It's just that, well, I've read your paper before, and, well, it's trash," he explained gently.

"Sure it's trash. People like to read trash, so what's the big deal? C'mon, I need the capital gains," he pleaded with a snide look at Al's cashmere overcoat.

"But, you see, I've made this commitment. I'm in this group that—well, the truth is, I just don't believe Jesus would read that stuff."

"You what?" the youth demanded incredulously.

"I'm trying to decide what Jesus would do," Al explained. "It's this pact I've made."

"Man, this sounds way out. What are you into?"

"Look, it's cold out here; I need to get back to work. If you're really interested, I'll buy you lunch and tell you while we eat."

"Best offer I've had all day," was the reply. A row of straight white teeth showed through the shaggy beard.

"What's your name? Mine's Al. Al Bonnell."

"I'm Joe. And would you believe, I'm from Kokomo?"

While Joe was doing justice to Mamma Mia's meatballs and spaghetti, Al managed to stuff down his linguini and talk simultaneously.

"And you think this is the way to real happiness?" Joe asked when Al had finished his explanation.

"Well, that's not really our motive, but Jesus did say that He wanted to give us an abundant life. Before you could try the experiment, you'd have to know Jesus, His teachings, and His principles. What do you really know about Him?"

"I saw the movie *Jesus Christ Superstar*. I had a course in comparative religions at the university. That's about the extent of my religious background."

"Have you ever read the New Testament?"

"Never even held one in my hands."

"If I buy you one, will you read it?"

"I guess so. You've got my curiosity up. I've never seen anyone as enthusiastic about religion as you are."

"OK, let's stop at the dime store," Al suggested with a glance at the clock. He was eager to get back to work on improving the inquiry portion of the system, but he believed Jesus would be more concerned with this contact with Joe.

In the store they chose a modern translation paperback New Testament. The colorful cover and sharp layout seemed to appeal to the open-minded youth.

"Thanks, Al. Thanks a lot. I'll read some of it this week; when I work your street again next Monday, I'll have lots of questions for you."

"It's a date," Al replied and hurried back to his computer.

By the time the boys were due home from school, Heather had finished her cleaning. Having the house "ready for inspection" usually made her feel secure and content, as if she were fulfilling her function in life, but today she still felt down. What was she going to do with the rest of the week? Wait for the dust to fall?

Don still hadn't called. Of course he wasn't particularly high on telephones; she was the one that was addicted.

This restlessness is ridiculous, she told herself. *It's this decision thing, I know it is! I never realized before how very few decisions I make. Nothing important. Is that it, Lord? I want something important to do. For You. But what? Surely I have some worthwhile outlet for the abilities You've given me. But where? What shall I do?*

I remember Josh said something the other night about the decisions he and Jackie made were mostly routine medical ones. Routine? He doesn't know the meaning of the word. At least they are involved in helping people. The hospital is full of people who need them.

At that moment the emergency ward at Holy Name Hospital was a mass of confusion. An old farm truck had plowed into the back of a city bus. Most of the bus passengers were more scared than hurt, though many of them had received cuts and bruises and quite a few had lost teeth when they were slammed against the metal seats in front of them. The truck driver, who was the most seriously injured, had been taken up to the operating room.

"In here next, doctor," the stout nurse called to Joshua Pittman, as she bustled toward one of the treatment rooms. A square-faced, dark-skinned elderly woman with two long, thick braids hanging down her back was sitting anxiously on a stool next to the examining table where a small, wide-eyed child sat.

"They don't speak English," the nurse commented as Josh walked toward the little girl who was staring stoically into space while sucking on the end of her long hair.

"Well, get someone who can translate. This woman looks as if she could use some reassuring," he ordered as he tenderly pulled back the tangled black hair that dangled in the child's face.

"*Hmmmm*, that's quite a cut you have there, sweetie. We'll have to fix that up for you. Nurse?" As the nurse set out the equipment, Josh tried to lay the child down. The girl stiffened defiantly and tried to pull away.

"My, you're a strong one for such a skinny little kid," Josh chuckled as he ran his hands gently down her arms and legs and checked for broken bones. He felt her ribs and then took his stethoscope to listen intently to her chest, front and back.

"Well, you can't be in too bad shape if you have that much fight left in you." Suddenly a look of concern crossed his dark face as he realized the child had never looked at him. She was still staring vacantly over his shoulder.

Slowly he passed his hand in front of her eyes. No reaction. Then, after the third time, instead of following his hand as expected, she looked him in the eye with a quizzical expression. Something in the depths of those huge black eyes struck a familiar chord. A lonely, hopeless emptiness dwelt at the bottom of those deep pools—an emptiness he had seen only in extremely old people. He felt an overwhelming urge to hold her close.

Gently he picked her up and held her. "It's all right, baby. We'll take good care of you. Nothing is going to hurt you. We'll protect you," he crooned to her.

"Doctor," the nurse bristled indignantly, "she doesn't understand you. She's getting blood on your clean coat. You . . .."

Josh shot the nurse a glance that stopped her as abruptly as if he had slapped her.

"Everything is going to be fine," he continued telling the child as he felt her relaxing in his arms. "We're going to take good care of you." Tenderly he laid her unprotesting form on the examining table.

"I'll want a complete set of x-rays," he ordered the nurse as he shone a light in the child's eyes. "Including a skull series. I don't think she's in bad shape, but we'll keep her overnight for observation."

"You asked for someone who speaks Spanish?" A vivacious young brunette in the uniform of a student nurse stood in the doorway.

"Yes. Explain to this woman that the child is going to be all right, but we want to keep her overnight," he demanded as he nodded toward the frightened old woman who sat wringing her hands. And I'd like to know something about this child. What's her name?"

The young student squatted down beside the elderly woman and took the work-worn hands in hers. *"Esta bien,"* she began softly.

While they talked, Josh worked swiftly. He applied butterfly stitches to the gash in the small forehead.

"Her name is Teresa. This is her grandmother," the student explained. "They live on a farm just off Highway 68."

"Really?" Josh questioned. "I didn't realize we had migrant farmers around here."

"Oh my, yes. A lot of these people live on the farms just north of here," the elderly nurse pontificated. "They don't do much migrating anymore—something to do with the immigration laws. They work the farms year-round."

"And I thought that was such an exclusive neighborhood. You learn something every day."

After the emergency was over, Josh headed toward the staff doctor's lounge for a cup of coffee. As he walked along, he thought of Teresa's reaction to his holding her and the way her muscles had relaxed and her breathing had slowed. In a rather delayed reaction he realized he had pulled a real "Jackie" with the child. Giving affection was part of his wife's philosophy of therapy.

Waiting for the elevator, Josh remembered the first time he had ever seen Jackie—back when she was still a student nurse and he was the newly appointed addition to the pediatric staff. Well, it wasn't really the first time he had seen her—just the first time he had noticed her.

While he passed the preemie nursery, he had observed an unauthorized addition to the staff in there, a young black woman in the striped uniform of a student. He knocked on the glass; when she looked up at him, he had motioned her into the hall.

"What are you doing in there at this time of the day?" he had demanded.

"I'm talking to that baby," she had replied as if that were a perfectly natural excuse.

"Talking to that baby? What do you mean, talking to that baby?" he had asked incredulously. "Talking to that preemie won't help pull it through."

"Well, it can't hurt," she had retorted with her black eyes flashing. "My grandmother talks to plants. They grow for her even if they were dying for someone else. If plants respond to sweet talk, why can't a baby?"

"Our ancestors also believed in voodoo," Josh had retorted. "Do you suggest we also make that a part of our treatments?"

"Oh!" she had snorted indignantly. She looked as though not stamping her foot took all the discipline she could muster. "That certainly isn't a fair equation, Doctor," she snapped haughtily. "And I'm going to continue to talk to that child and pray for it. I'm going to get every other nurse I can to do the same."

Josh had had to smile at her intensity. She didn't even have enough sense to know that a student nurse was supposed to be not arguing but quaking in her soft-soled shoes when one of the residents such as himself spoke to her!

"Just what are you telling that miniscule bit of humanity?" he asked as he tried not to let his amusement show.

"I'm telling her that her mommy and daddy love her very much and they want her to live. I say she is beautiful and that even though her body is very tiny, it is perfect and she should fight to live," she had replied. "And I'd really like to know her name."

"We usually suggest that the parents don't name a child that has no more chance of making it than this one has. She's nearly two-and-a-half months premature," he had explained as he tried convince the determined young woman how hopeless her attentions were. "She weighs less than two pounds. Her chances are very slim."

"I don't care. I'm going to try anyway," she had declared with a snap of her head that threatened to dislodge her cap. Then she had turned on her heel to go ask the mother whether a name had been selected.

Josh had decided then that he was going to find out more about that spunky gal—that gal who soon had most of the nurses in pediatrics praying for and talking to tiny Lynne Anne. Lynne Anne must be a teen-ager now. She still held the record for the smallest baby ever to survive at Holy Name Hospital.

The elevator door slid open; Josh returned to the present. He'd have to tell Jackie about Teresa. Perhaps they could stop by and see her before they left work.

The rest of the day Heather had been busy with the boys, but now they were in bed and the house was quiet again. Don still wasn't home—hadn't even called to say when to expect him to be home.

She wandered into the family room and picked up the television guide. She had a great choice: she either could watch the last half of a movie, a pro basketball game, or a doctor show that had been on for so many years that even the new programs seemed like reruns.

"Guess I'll read something," she decided. "That's it! I'll reread *In His Steps*. I haven't read it in years. Maybe I'll get some suggestions . . . if I can find it."

She walked to the towering bookcase to the left of the fireplace where she kept Christian books. Don had despaired when he learned her "system" for arranging them. They were placed not according to topic, title, or author, but by color. For Heather, fitting books into the decor was more important than easy accessibility.

The problem was, she hadn't read the book in so long, she wasn't sure what color it was. A dull orange? At last she spied it on the second from the top shelf. A dark brown.

She climbed on a small wooden footstool to reach it, took it down, and carried it along to the kitchen. She opened a cupboard and searched for a snack so she could read and munch at the same time. With a book and food she didn't feel quite so lonely.

Chapter 7

After she completed her Tuesday morning chores, Heather continued reading *In His Steps*. By 11:30 she had finished. *Well, it may be antiquated*, she decided, as she put the book on the glass-topped coffee table, *but it is still certainly thought-provoking.*

Those people thought they could change the world. I certainly don't have any illusions about that, but I could change myself some. First off, I could quit being so pig-headed and invite Don back to our room. I've really been convicting him on circumstantial evidence anyway. How could anyone with such a boyishly innocent face be guilty of anything? I'll call him right now," she decided and walked toward the phone on the desk.

And what about Wanda? Maybe I've been unfair to her, too. I never have really been very friendly to her. She lives all alone. I doubt if she could have any real type of relationship with her charges. She even sits by herself in church every Sunday. I'll call her too and invite her to lunch tomorrow.

She punched out Don's number but got a busy signal. She then realized she didn't have Wanda's number and couldn't think of the long, fancy title of the home where Wanda worked. No one ever used the cumbersome name, but it would be listed that way in the phone book. She decided to call Sheila, the church secretary. Sheila should have the number.

"Community Church," Sheila answered with a lilt in her voice.

"Hi, Sheila, this is Heather. Do you have a phone number for Wanda Hendricks? I don't know how to find it in the book."

"Yes, we have that information in our files," was the professional-sounding reply. Then in a quieter voice Sheila said, "Pastor is just leaving with the president of the school board.

"Yeah, here it is. It's really about all we do know about her," she said in her more normal, gossipy voice. "All I know is that when she joined the church, she came on 'statement of faith' from a church somewhere in Minnesota. I would really love to have the lowdown on our lady of mystery!"

"She doesn't offer much information about herself, does she?" Heather agreed.

"I should say not. I've wondered whether she is secretly working for the CIA or something. I'll tell you one thing, though," Sheila volunteered conspiratorially, "she's been invited to dinner by a number of families but never asked back twice. The husbands find her all too fascinating. I've even known some people attempt to do a little matchmaking, but she seems to have no interest in single men!"

"That does seem unusual."

"Unusual? Is that ever an understatement! You'd think a gal as good-looking as she is would have a man of her own by now. Maybe she's divorced or something. I do know how old she is," Sheila confided. "At least, according to what she put on her membership card, she is now 26."

"Very interesting," Heather said with tongue in cheek. This kind of gossip was not the information she needed. "How about that phone number?" she asked.

"Oh, of course. 879-3232."

"Thanks. See you Sunday."

Heather wrote the number on the back of her phone book and then punched out the number.

"879-3232," answered an impersonal voice. "May I help you?"

"I'd like to speak to Miss Wanda Hendricks, please."

"I'm sorry, but Miss Hendricks just left for a luncheon appointment. Would you like to leave a number?"

"Oh, no. Thank you."

Heather tried Don's number again. This time Alice answered.

"Sorry, Mrs. Novak, but he just left for lunch."

"Oh, *phoo*. I tried before, but the line was busy."

"Yes, he had a long conversation with someone, which is very rare for him. You know how he dislikes talking over the phone. I got the impression that he was meeting whoever he had been talking to at Brady's. Wanted to get there early before the crowd."

"OK. Thank you, Alice. Bye."

Heather hung up slowly. *Wanda just left for lunch. Don just left for lunch. A coincidence, surely. Besides, he's gone to Brady's. He wouldn't take her there. That's our place!*

The more she thought about the possibility of the two of them being together, the more tormented she became. She wished again that he wasn't quite so good-looking. It was not easy being married to a tall, fair-haired Adonis, although she had to admit he was as popular with men as he was with women. He always maintained he wasn't a flirt; he was just friendly to everyone.

She felt like chewing nails. If she hadn't just stripped and waxed the floor the day before, she would mop it. She needed some physical outlet to vent her anger.

I must get out of this house! she decided. *But Jesus wouldn't dash down there like a fool and check up on a supposedly wayward husband. I shouldn't go, but I can't stand wondering about it anymore.*

She pulled on her boots, coat, and hat. With a quick dash of lipstick she was off. Brady's was between their home and the car lot, so she figured she would have plenty of time to get there before Don and his luncheon date were through eating.

When she arrived, the parking lot was overflowing, so she parked in a supermarket lot across the street. She dodged the cars that honked at her as she flew through the lot.

Pulling open the heavy wooden door of the restaurant she found the waiting area crowded. She squirmed her way toward the entrance, where she could look down into the restaurant at the patrons who were already seated. She could barely make out the heads of those who were seated in booths lined against the wall, but there to her right was Don.

He was flashing his toothy smile while he made some kind of extreme gesture. Then he leaned forward to make a point to his blonde companion. Thick, long blonde waves nodded in agreement.

Heather felt sick—as though someone had kicked her in the stomach. She grabbed the wrought-iron railing in front of her as she tried to control herself. *I didn't really believe it. I didn't want to believe it. I've got to get out of here. I can't—*

Just then Don's eyes looked up and caught hers. He blinked in surprise. Then a smile of real pleasure crept over his face. He rose from his seat and moved toward her. Motioning to the hostess that she was with him, he took her by the hand and led her down the four steps into the room.

"Heather! What a delightful surprise. You haven't come to have lunch with me since the first snow." He gave her hand a little squeeze and, with his other hand gently on the middle of her back, led her to his table.

Her mind was in a whirl. The gears didn't seem to be meshing correctly. Automatically her feet responded to Don's leading; she found herself at his booth.

"I want you to meet a new friend of mine, Heather." The tall, long-haired youth arose and extended his hand to her. "This is Greg Walters. He called about a job this morning, but we got to talking about the experiment our group is trying. You can help me explain our ground rules."

Heather flashed her dimples and sank gratefully into Don's side of the booth. "I am very glad to meet you, Greg," she sighed with great sincerity.

After they finished lunch, Greg waved goodbye to them and left for the office to fill out an application.

"Where are you parked?" Don asked Heather. "I'll walk you to your car."

"Across the street," she replied contentedly as she felt him take her hand. Together they made their way across the busy thoroughfare.

"Well, when was I forgiven?" he asked with a twinkle in his eyes.

"When you smiled at me," she confided as she snuggled into the arm he had halfway around her.

"When I smiled," he repeated. His brows raised quizzically. "What do you mean?"

"In Brady's, when you first noticed me, you gave me that big, special smile that means you like me—you want me. That's all I really need to make me happy, Don. To feel I'm important to you."

"Oh, you goose!" He laughed. "Of course you are important to me." He drew her close and gave her a long, hungry kiss. A whistle from a carry-out boy made them realize where they were.

"Let's get in the car," Don suggested. "I thought you might have broken down and read the newspaper or something," he continued when they were huddled inside.

"The newspaper?"

"Yes. If you had watched the news last Friday night or read the papers the next morning, you would have discovered the January thaw had caused the Des Plaines River to flood. They had to evacuate people from their homes and everything. It knocked out most of the phones around here. We didn't get our service restored until this morning."

"A flood?" Heather repeated numbly.

"Yes, a flood. The biggest mess you ever saw. The service department is higher than the show room, though you can't tell it to look at it, and the water was running through. It got everything full of grease and oil and guck and seeped into the carpeted section of the building. I couldn't just leave it. We stayed and fought a losing battle until the National Guard stopped by and helped us sandbag the place.

"I was so beat by the time I got home. Then you pretended to be asleep and wouldn't let me explain."

"But—but, it was so late. Why did you bother Wanda by exchanging cars at that hour? You couldn't have waited until morning."

"Bothered Wanda? I didn't bother Wanda; I didn't even see her. I just parked her car and then drove off in mine. That didn't take any time at all!"

"But what about the keys?"

"Oh, I had given her the extra key I keep hidden under the hood, since I didn't know what time I would be by. She did the same. We swapped them at church Sunday."

"Oh," Heather mumbled as she realized how incorrectly she had added circumstances.

"You mean you thought I was with Wanda? Oh, Heather," he moaned as he pulled his wife close to him. "I've told you you have no reason to be jealous of her. Something about Wanda seems very—I don't know—sad. I'm glad when she smiles, because she needs to for her own good. But that is all!

She has no romantic designs on me, I can assure you.

"I love you, Heather. Can't you believe that?" he pleaded as he kissed her forehead, her eyes, her cheek, her lips. "I love you so much. I get tied in knots when you put me in the deep-freeze. I feel so—so defensive. Can't you realize how much I need to believe you're on my side—?"

"Oh, I'm on your side," Heather responded with tears streaming down her cheeks. "I'm sorry, Don. So sorry. I feel like a fool. If you're forgive me, I'll try, I'll really try not to ever be jealous again."

"Of course I forgive you. But next time, please, let's talk about it, OK?"

"Of course." She nodded.

"And now I have to leave you," he murmured as he kissed her gently on the lips. Again. And again. "And I really don't feel like it."

"Good!" She grinned.

"But I'll sure be home as early as I can tonight."

"Oh, but I have to babysit for Sally Ann tonight," she reminded him.

"Oh, that's right," he remembered disappointedly. "And you surely couldn't break that promise. Well, at least you've learned the secret." He grinned. "The sweeter, more lovin' you are, the earlier I get home."

He gave her one last kiss in parting and started back to work. When he arrived, he found that Greg had already filled out the necessary forms and had left with a promise to call in the next day. He went into his office and plopped down in his chair without even removing his hat and coat.

He glanced at his watch. The twins wouldn't be home for two-and-a half hours. At this time of day he could be home in 30 minutes. He picked up the phone.

"Hello," Heather answered brightly.

"Hi, gorgeous. How about a date?"

"Well, sure, Don. When?" she asked with a smile in her voice.

"Just as soon as I get there," he replied.

"What? Now?"

"If it's OK with you."

"I'll be waiting."

He strode out of the office and announced to his secretary, "Alice, I'm taking the afternoon off."

"What?" she asked with open-mouthed wonder. "But you never—"

"I know I never. But I can always start sometime."

The secretary nodded in agreement. She was amazed at how completely delighted with himself he seemed.

Chapter 8

Heather floated through the next couple of days on a bright, shiny cloud of love. She felt like a bride again. Don not only called her twice on Wednesday, he brought home flowers.

Maybe my place in life is just as a contented wife and mother, she decided while she made doughnuts in anticipation of the Thursday-evening meeting. *Could my great desire to "do" something have happened just so I'd have something impressive to report to The Group tonight? If so, that was a pretty poor motive, wasn't it, Lord?*

Well, I am now willing to do or be whatever You want. I'll be content to make Don and the boys happy and to continue working with my Sunday-school class. If there's anything else You want of me, I'll wait for You to show me.

"This is really remarkable," she exclaimed later as The Group settled down in the family room. "I mean, this has to be the first time everyone arrived early!"

"Yeah," Kenny agreed, "you'd almost think we were all eager to hear what's happened this week."

"Well, I looked up some background information on the book *In His Steps* at the library this week," Jan explained as she pulled some photocopies from a folder she had on her lap. "Would you like to begin with this?" She glanced up from her Indian-like position on the floor to those around her. Everyone seemed to agree, so she continued.

"Charles Sheldon was a Congregational minister in Topeka, KS. He got the inspiration for the book while he was resting one hot summer day back in 1896. He read it a chapter at a time to the young people of his church. At the same time a religious weekly, called the *Chicago Advance*, began publishing it as a series. For some unknown reason, the publisher only filed one copy with the copyright each week, instead of two as the law required.

"Because of this goof, the book went into the public domain. No one, including the author, had legal ownership of it. Sixteen different publishers in America and 50 in Europe and Australia published editions of the book. Naturally they could sell it cheaply, since they didn't pay the author any royalties."

"What! No commission?" Don exploded. "That doesn't seem fair. Couldn't he have sued or something?"

"I guess not," Jan replied, "but I really don't think he would have even if he had the legal right, because it was this 'mistake' that made his the best-selling religious novel of all time. I get the impression he was grateful that so many people were challenged and inspired by his work.

"This was back in the days of amillennialism when many theologians taught that the world was going to get better and better. He lived until two days before his 89th birthday in 1946, still believing the standards of conduct Jesus taught would someday be accepted by the entire human race."

"That seems rather naive considering that two world wars erupted after the writing of the book," Wanda commented.

"Yes, the world was certainly changed during this century," Josh agreed, "but I took time to read the book this week. I still found it challenging."

"Challenging!" Al interrupted. "I think it's more than just challenging. It works! I just can't wait any longer. I've got to tell you about this young guy I 'accidentally' met on Monday," he exclaimed. He went into minute detail about his encounter with the young street radical. "And he left with his New Testament. He called out, 'I'll see you next week.'"

"Oh, how exciting!" Jackie exclaimed as she clapped her hands. "Do you think he'll really show?"

"Better than that," Al continued. "When I left work yesterday, there he was. He was standing outside my building with the biggest, most beautiful grin I've ever seen. He had spent the past two days reading the entire New Testament. He greeted me with, 'Man, I didn't know Jesus was really the Son of God! And I sure never heard that God loved me. This is the greatest!'

"I was so excited, I was about to flip," Al continued breathlessly. "I had to meet Jan at the terminal, so I didn't know what else to do but invite him home with me. Besides, I really wanted her in on the conversation."

"And they had a lot of conversation!" Jan interjected. "We talked all the way home, during supper, and on into the wee hours of the night. He spent the night with us. We talked all the way back into town. By the time I got to the library, I was hoarse."

"But he really has had an experience with the Lord," Al added. "Just from reading the Bible! No preacher, nobody trying to pressure him or anything. It's the neatest thing I've ever seen! I mean, it seems like a real miracle to me!"

"Every conversion is a real miracle," Heather commented.

"Yeah, sure," Al agreed. "But I was in on this one! It's the most thrilling thing I've ever seen. Why, his whole attitude has changed; you'd hardly know he was the same person. We'd have brought him tonight, but we got him in contact with a Christian group on his campus. They meet tonight, too. He wanted to get in with some Christians in his peer group."

"Well, I'm afraid the rest of this meeting is going to seem kinda tame," Kenny drawled. "Nobody's gonna be able to top that."

Amid murmurs of agreement, Al put up his hand in a request to continue. "I have something I need to add, though," he said seriously. "I haven't even told Jan about this, but I really feel I need to say it.

"It's about—Well, it's such a little thing that it sounds rather dumb, but I still have to say it. It's that piece of gum wrapper I went back and picked up. If I hadn't done that—if I hadn't listened to the inner voice that told me to pick it up, even if someone might see me and think I was weird—I never would have met Joe. That gum wrapper brought me to just the right place at the right time."

"That's not dumb, Al," Heather said softly. "That's obedience. Obedience in small things is a lesson we all need to learn."

A thoughtful silence fell on the group.

Then Josh shifted forward in his seat and with head lowered cleared his throat. "That's the most significant thing that's been said," the tall pediatrician said slowly. "Obedience in small things is just the lesson I need. All too often I go forth with such great self-confidence that I tend to rely completely on myself and my own wisdom. I forget that my knowledge is limited. I need to ask for guidance in the medical decisions I make.

"However," he added as if he had just thought of it, "I did have one experience this week that was a little unusual. I encountered a little girl—a little Hispanic girl named Teresa, who had been in a wreck. Something about her—her eyes, I guess, compelled me to pick her up, hold her close, and try to comfort her.

"I—I don't know what significance that has," he said, rather apologetically. "It's just that I don't usually take the time to do such things."

"Ahh, time," Heather sighed. "Maybe time and obedience are all interwoven some way."

"I can see that," Don agreed. "The priorities we set on our time can sometimes preclude obedience. Sins of omission, that kind of thing."

"I've found I have lots of time," Heather confessed. "As a matter of fact, I've realize that most days the biggest decision I make is what I shall eat next." She paused, expecting The Group to laugh, but when no one did, she looked around rather bewilderedly. "I—I feel a need for some decisions I could make. So I could use my time more profitably. Any suggestions?"

"Well," Josh replied thoughtfully, "you could go visit Teresa. She doesn't live far from here. Her grandmother might appreciate someone visiting and changing bandages for her. She doesn't speak English, but you majored in Spanish in college or something, didn't you?"

"I minored in it," Heather admitted hesitantly, "but I haven't used it for years. I certainly don't think I could communicate about medical matters."

"It was just a thought," Josh said. "The grandmother seemed as if she could use a friend."

"I will admit one thing, though," Heather continued as she dismissed the subject. "I've noticed a change in my attitude this week. I'll have to confess that I was a little perturbed when Don invited you back for this week. All I thought of was 'more work for me.' But I've decided that since the Lord has allowed us to have this beautiful home, I can certainly be willing to use it for Him whenever I find the opportunity. Also, I've found that really trying to live as Jesus would has improved my relationship with Don."

"It sure has!" Don added enthusiastically with such an open, frank grin at Heather that she began blushing.

"Oh, Don!" she wailed in embarrassment. She hated the flushed warmth she felt in her face.

Amid the companionable laughter of The Group, Sally Ann rushed to her friend's defense. "It does make a difference," she declared. "Kenny has been much more considerate this week. I've found myself trying more diligently to please him. When each of us is trying to please the other, something beautiful happens."

Don started to add a remark, but he realized how serious Sally Ann was and decided to stop teasing.

"She's right," Kenny continued. "I've done some tall thinkin' this week about all the time I spend entertaining people without really being much help to them. I want to become more involved with people. Perhaps more important, I want Sally Ann involved with me. We've discovered a lot of folks have backgrounds similar to ours and that who now live in the city. But most of them are havin' a much tougher time adjusting than we are. We want to help.

"Numerous church groups work with these people. So do boys' clubs, Scouts, and the Y. But they need volunteers. I have the time during off-season. We both believe we should do what we can. It'll mean the loss of the income I make from speaking, but that really isn't much. Besides, neither of us is used to livin' high off the hog. We can scrape by on what the team pays me." He grinned.

"I think the fact that you can use your fame to help others is great," Don commented.

"Aw, I don't know how famous I am," Kenny replied with genuine embarrassment.

"Sure you're famous," Jackie quipped. "But don't worry. None of us is too impressed." Kenny laughed with the rest and felt more at ease.

"We can really relate to what you are saying about becoming involved with your people, though," Jackie continued. "We've felt the same way. We're concerned about the lack of 'color' in our neighborhood. As you know, we even had to send our son away to a private school so he could have an opportunity to make friends among his own people."

"This is one way in which we disagreed with the characters in the book," Josh commented. "They felt they should go down and live among the lower classes, but I firmly believe the ghetto doesn't need any more people. What we'd like to do is help some of the ghetto people move out to the nice neighborhoods in the suburbs. So we did a little investigating over the weekend."

"Yeah, Saturday we made the rounds of the local real-estate offices." Jackie laughed, a look of satisfaction on the well-chiseled features of her face. "Man, that was some fun! We'd walk into an office and watch the cold sweat break out on those honkies' faces. Without even finding out anything about us, they would start giving us the run-around. I was really tempted to give them a tough time—you know, tell them we were ready to move in with our 15 kids or something, but Josh made me play it straight."

"Seriously," Josh interrupted, "we discovered some disturbing facts. Despite the Civil Rights Act of 1968, Title VII, which prohibited racial discrimination in the sale of private housing, not one black person owns property in our suburb."

"But you live there," Jan said.

"We rent," Josh explained, "from a very unusual landlady. But the real-estate people seem to have a practice called 'steering', which encourages minority groups to seek housing in certain areas. They have a system of coding the applicants' race on their office forms. You can become rather suspicious."

Everyone nodded in agreement.

"Well, Jackie and I don't have much time to devote; we

don't have off-seasons in medical work, but we do have a little money. And some influential friends. What we'd like to do is help give blacks already working in factories and businesses in the community opportunity to find housing closer to their work. I'm appalled at how much 'reverse commuting' is going on. And it is expensive; these people should not have to devote so much of their salaries to transportation!"

"I'd never really thought about that before, Josh," Don mused, "but I have four black mechanics working in my service department. I'm not sure where they live, but I know it's nowhere nearby."

"That sounds like a natural," Josh exclaimed. "We are looking for stable families with secure positions. We want them to prove a real asset to the community."

"Well, Hank has been with me for seven years. Has a fine wife and two teen-age sons. They come to company Christmas parties and our summer picnics and fit right in. They are really fine, dependable people. If you'd like to meet them and my other black employees, I'd be glad to set it up."

"Fine," Josh answered. "We'll give that top priority this week."

"And if any of them want to move, I'll certainly do all I can to help," Don added.

"Oh, but this discussion is frustrating me all over again," Heather wailed. "All week I've felt that if Jesus were living my life, He would find something to do for others. But what? My life seems so easy; I just drift along. Yet I know that the world has so many needs. Surely I should do something to help."

"I've been thinking along those same lines," Al confided. "And I've concluded that before I can do anything for the Lord, I first have to be something. I have to be totally dedicated and be willing to do whatever He wants me to—even if that means giving up my computer."

"Give up your computer!" Heather exclaimed. "Why would He want you to give up your computer?"

"I don't know that He does, but I do think I should be willing. I have to admit, I am really hung up on that machine. I love it. That might be tough for you to understand, but it's true. See, I've spent nearly three years setting the design for our project. We're just now beginning implementation. The grind is making the system function—teaching it to do what you want it to. Well, now we're beginning the fun part: watching our creation produce.

"Computers are addicting! Really, one easily can become totally absorbed with them. The project I'm involved with now is compiling all scientific information in one data base. One day it will be of great benefit to all humanity. I really believe it. But would Jesus be content to dedicate His specialized ability to this goal?"

"Next Al's going to explain to us just how brilliant he is," Jan teased. "All geniuses are so modest."

"I'll be modest some other time," he answered seriously. "Right now I'm trying to share my dilemma. I believe I could use this special ability I have with computers to help in Bible translation. I've believed this ever since I took a graduate course in formal linguistics at IIT. Just think, if I could set up a computer that would help translators break down unwritten languages, I could save at least a year on each translation. And translators work in hundreds of tribes."

"Could you really do that?" Wanda asked.

"Save one year? Oh, easy. That's a very conservative figure, because computers could help in every step of the process, not just learning the language but in the actual translation and in getting ready for publication."

"But it would mean leaving the computer you love so

much here," Heather commented softly. "And you're really willing to do this?"

"Well, I don't even know if they want me." Al laughed. "But I felt compelled to offer my services. I wrote to the Bible Translators headquarters this afternoon and mailed the letter on my way over here."

"What do you think about this, Jan?" Wanda asked.

"What can I say? If he's willing to give up his computer, I sure can give up the library. And as long as the mails are running, I could write from any place in the world. We could be sent somewhere where I'd have trouble getting resource material, but I'll worry about that when the time comes."

"I think I can understand how difficult that decision was for you, Al," Heather commented. "Don, would you be willing to give up your business?"

"Me? Sure," Don replied easily. "I'm a salesman by disposition, but cars aren't really that important to me."

Amid murmurs of agreement, Heather shook her head. "I don't, I couldn't, I just don't know if I would be willing to give up my house," she confessed. "I thought I had come a long way by being willing to have meetings here. But give it up? I don't know."

"Don't feel too badly," Wanda consoled her. "I'm having problems being willing myself. I found that making the decisions that crop up in my daily routine as I felt Jesus would make them was not too difficult. I was perhaps more kind with some of my charges. I had more patience with some people who imposed on my time off than I usually would have had; but as a lifetime principle, it's another thing. If you're really serious about it, you are soon confronted with some life-changing decisions."

"I sure found that out," Al interrupted.

"So have some of the rest of us," Kenny added.

"But I'm still rebellious about something," Wanda admitted. "I wish you'd pray for me."

Heather looked into Wanda's clear, green eyes as the woman made this request. For the first time she saw the lost little-girl look that Don had mentioned. Wanda was so very beautiful, yet she seemed very vulnerable.

"Well, what's our conclusion?" Kenny asked. "Has our experiment worked, or should we try it for another week, or what?"

"I've concluded that, once you get started, you can't very well stop," Al ventured.

"I agree," Don added. "I've become concerned with the integrity of my salesmen, the efficiency of the repair department, and even the honesty of our advertisements. I just couldn't forget about these things now, but what repercussions these decisions will have is another problem. What develops will take time. I might lose a lot of business. A couple of salesmen are very peeved with me already. I don't know what will happen, but I'm determined to stick with it."

"You're right," Jackie agreed. "No telling what trouble we might get ourselves into. I'm for reporting to each other again next week."

"But next week the whole group meets," Heather cautioned.

"Why not let them in on it?" Kenny asked. "Where do we meet anyway?"

"The Lindholms' house. I vote for telling about the experiment. Some of them might think we've become fanatics, but others will want to join with us."

With this agreed on, everyone rose to leave. Heather made her way to Wanda's side and hesitantly asked, "Would you like to visit my home for lunch one day?"

"Oh, Heather. Would I ever!" She responded so enthusiastically that Heather was a little overwhelmed. "I've wanted to talk with you," Wanda continued. "A couple of times last week I almost called and invited myself over."

"How about tomorrow, then?"

"Fine. I'll be looking forward to it."

"So will I."

Chapter 9

"I really believe I owe you an apology," Wanda said, as she seated herself before the fancy salad Heather had prepared for lunch. "The very first time I met you, I had the strongest impression that you could be a friend. A very good friend. So I have gone out of my way the past year to avoid you as much as possible."

"I—I really don't understand," Heather replied with a quizzical tilt of her curly head. "You didn't want to be my friend?"

"I haven't wanted to be anyone's friend. Not for a long time. That's what's bothering me. This past week I've been tormented by the realization of the strong wall I've built around myself. I've been secretive and aloof and uncaring—the very opposite of how Jesus would live my life."

"Well, I'm willing to be your friend." Heather hesitated as she picked at her salad. "But I really don't know what to say. How can I help?"

"Being my friend is the biggest help—just listening to me. I've had enough psychology to know I need to talk to someone. *Confide* would be a better word. Last week I thought of calling Pastor Wilkes, but I just couldn't; I needed a woman friend. I wanted to call you, but I've been so cold to you that I was afraid you might reject me."

"I have some confessing to do, too," Heather admitted. "I felt very impressed to invite you over before, but I rejected the idea. I was having some hang-ups of my own. But that's all over; now I feel I can be an understanding listener. And I can assure you that though I have many faults, gossiping isn't one of them."

"I know." Wanda smiled. "I've noticed. Well, the only way I know to start is to tell you something about my family. I was reared in a small town not far from Minneapolis. My parents had both lived there all their lives. They went to high school and college together and married soon after graduation. My dad inherited a small general store which he modernized and made profitable. They used to joke that Dad ran the store and Mom ran Dad." She smiled nostalgically.

"My brother Buddy was just 12 months and two days older than I. He was named William after my father, but we all called him Buddy. He was my first and best friend. Most of my early childhood memories center around him. I used to follow him everywhere. He tolerated my presence with unusual patience.

"I guess it was trying to keep up with Buddy that made me such a tomboy. I was always getting cut or scratched or banged up some way. My mother despaired at trying to make me look like a dainty little lady, so she let me run around in blue jeans except on Sundays.

"On Sunday we all had to dress in our best. Mother always wore a hat to church. We lived only three-and-a-half blocks from our church. I can remember on warm spring days skipping along carrying my Bible and Sunday-school quarterly. We must have looked like Norman Rockwell characters stepping from the pages of the *Saturday Evening Post*. Does it sound too corny to say we had a wholesome life?"

"It doesn't sound corny to me at all," Heather commented. "It sounds like a secure, loving childhood."

"Yeah," Wanda sighed as she flipped back the long tresses that had fallen in front of her shoulders. "Everything seemed like such fun back then. Perhaps it was Buddy. He had the ability of making everything seem so exciting. All of life was a challenge to him. In my mind I can't conjure up a boyhood picture of him standing still. He seemed always to be running, jumping, climbing, laughing. Always laughing.

"He had pale, blond unruly curls, which he detested. Every kid in town knew better than to tease him about that. And celestial blue eyes. A rather strange thing about his eyes: when he smiled, they seemed to shine on you.

"Then when we were 9 and 10, David was born. We were all delighted, especially Dad, because this son had his dark hair and eyes. To Buddy and me, David seemed rather like the pet we could never have because our mother was allergic to animal fur. As a baby he used to crawl after us all over our old-fashioned frame house.

"I even remember his first step." She smiled, a lovely glow spreading over her face. "We were all on the big porch that wrapped halfway around our home. Mom and Dad were sitting on the swing. Buddy and I were punching holes in a couple of jar lids, getting ready to catch some of the fireflies showing off in the yard.

"David pulled himself up awkwardly and held onto a straight-backed, cane-bottomed chair. Then halfway between us, a firefly glowed. David spotted it. Before he realized what he was doing, he took three tottering steps toward the insect.

"I squealed with glee and clapped my hands. That sort of startled him. He got the funniest look on his round little baby face—he was only 11 months old. He looked around, realized what he had done, and plopped down on his well-padded bottom.

"After that, his world expanded as he was allowed the run of our big fenced-in yard. Sometimes Buddy and I would even play with him in the sandbox we had more or less abandoned.

I remember we were always teaching him something Mother said was too hard for him. By the time he was 2, he knew all his colors, recognized all the letters in the alphabet, and could count things up to 10.

"He was really an exceptionally bright child. By the time he was 3, he could read easy little storybooks. Buddy and I were so proud of him; we enjoyed showing him off to our peers. He never was a rough, tough kind of boy, but my how he loved to read!

"Buddy and I had a passion for baseball. Since our community had no Little League teams organized then, no grownups said I couldn't play with the boys. And they knew better than try to exclude me. Besides, though Kenny might find this hard to believe, I could play as well as the rest of them," she said rather proudly.

"David was the team mascot and bat boy, which was really quite amusing because he wasn't much taller than the bats. But the summer he was 5, he became ill. Looking back now, I realize he had never been an exceptionally healthy child. He had always tired easily and bruised for no apparent reason.

"Finally our kindly old family doctor admitted he didn't know what to do for David and suggested that we take him for tests to a large medical facility not too far away. Even though I was nearly a teen-ager then, no one explained to me or Buddy just what the problem was. We were only told that there were complications. I had never heard of anyone dying of "complications", but from the way Mother staggered around the house in a daze we knew something was drastically wrong.

"Finally, after a couple of weeks, Dad took Buddy and me aside and talked with us. 'We have a difficult decision to make,' he told us. 'The doctors say we can leave David in the hospital where he will be surrounded by strangers, or we can bring him home to die in his own bed.'"

"Oh, no!" Heather cried out. "How tragic!"

"My sentiments exactly," Wanda replied coolly. Her green eyes were as emotionless as granite. "He explained how hard it would be to see David so sick. That's why he felt Buddy and I should have a voice in the decision.

"'I'll be waiting in the parlor,' he said. 'Take your time and be sure. If we bring him home, we will have to be brave. Brave and loving and kind. You'll have to help your mother.'"

"Oh, what a decision to have to make," Heather sympathized.

"Yes, it was very difficult. At first Buddy and I just clung to each other and sobbed. We couldn't believe it. Death was for old people, not little boys. We made the only decision possible; they brought him home."

Heather got up from the table to replace her soggy napkin. As she extracted a box of tissues from a drawer, she wondered how Wanda could keep her composure.

"So we watched our little mascot die," Wanda continued, when Heather returned to her chair. "He only lasted a week. He grew visibly thinner and weaker. Buddy read to him by the hour. The rest of us tried from time to time, but we would choke up and have to stop.

"At first Buddy read Mark Twain, but after a couple of days David asked him to read from his old Bible storybook he had read so many times. I remember, when Buddy came to the story about Jesus and the little children, David put his hand on Buddy's to stop him and asked weakly, 'I'm going to see Jesus, aren't I?' 'Yes,' Buddy replied simply. And David smiled.

"The next day, as we all hovered around his bed, David died. Attending his funeral was the hardest thing I had ever done in my life. The little white coffin was the most hideous, monstrous object I had ever seen. I couldn't understand why

God would allow such a thing to happen.

"After the burial, Buddy and I sat on the swing and listened to the adults in the house who clustered around our parents. 'It just doesn't seem fair,' I said. 'He didn't even get to go to school. He was looking forward to it so. Why couldn't God at least let him go to school?' I asked Buddy.

"His reply was really quite mature for a 13-year-old, I think. He said, 'If we just trust the Lord when things are fine, we must not have much faith. We have to trust Him and believe He will teach us to laugh again.' He was right, of course, but life was never quite the same. We had such an emptiness.

"My parents seemed to age quickly after David died. Within the year my mother turned gray; her walk changed. I don't know if I can explain it, but her footsteps seemed to drag; she slouched. She seemed to have lost her enthusiasm for life. *Defeated*, I think, is the word. She seemed utterly defeated.

"And she became a worrier—absolutely fanatical in her concern that Buddy or I might get hurt. When Buddy earned money for a motorcycle, she just would not hear of it. Dad agreed with her; no way would they allow him to have a cycle.

"They wouldn't even sign the release papers allowing Buddy to play on athletic teams at school. That was really hard for him, because he was 6-feet tall before he finished junior high. He was very good about it, though. He didn't beg or complain.

"Perhaps because he was forbidden to go out for team sports, he turned to hobbies. Hiking, biking, wild life, photography—he won honorable mention in a national photo contest when he was a high-school junior. He liked to make things, especially from wood. He even got Mother to teach him needlepoint and knitting. He seemed to want to learn everything.

"When he left for his freshman year in college, the house was so empty, even though he left behind a number of half-finished projects. He wrote us faithfully—at least once a week. Newsy chatty letters that sounded just like him. They helped bridge the gap.

"I had a steady boyfriend by then. I was a cheerleader, so I kept busy. But that year was the greatest Thanksgiving ever." She smiled. "Buddy was there. He filled me with talk of school until I could hardly wait to graduate and accompany him back to the campus.

"By this time he had decided to become a Bible translator for some primitive tribe—that's why I was so interested in Al's comments last night. But I think Buddy was attracted not only by the plight of the Bibleless cultures but by the very fact that going to these peoples would mean self-sacrifice. Danger and deprivation seemed to appeal to him. I remember he quoted Romans 12:1 to me, with special emphasis on presenting his body as a *living sacrifice.* He believed so strongly that this was the best way he could serve the Lord.

"The only thing that made his return to school easier for me was the realization that the Christmas break was just a few weeks away and that he would be returning home soon. Then, the Saturday before Christmas, the telephone rang. Buddy had been hit by a car; we needed to come immediately. Sand-wiched between my parents on the plane that took us to him, I learned at last the truth of the tragedy that stalked us. Hemo-philia."

"Hemophilia?" Heather questioned. "Doesn't that mean you bleed too profusely?"

"Yes. It's a genetically linked blood disorder. Males who inherit the disease can bleed to death from minor injuries because the blood-clotting mechanism of the blood doesn't function correctly. It seems ironic, but we had studied about blood diseases in health class shortly before, so I knew a little about it.

"But my poor mother. She kept saying, 'I didn't know. I didn't know.' She seemed to feel guilty, when of course it wasn't her fault. She had only one sister, a teacher who never married, and her mother had been an only child. I guess the generation before that just didn't know about the blood disorder, so it wasn't until David was hospitalized that she learned about it."

"Oh, how horrible for her," Heather said. "Then that's why she became so protective. And of course they couldn't let Buddy play sports or have a motorcycle; they knew any injury could prove fatal."

"Yes."

"But why hadn't they told you?"

"That's what I wanted to know. It sounds cruel now, but my initial reaction was anger. Mother was already crying copiously, but I lashed out at her and demanded to know why we hadn't been warned. Dad slipped his arm around me and whispered hoarsely, 'Buddy knew, sweetheart. He knew all along, He was the one who insisted that you not be told.'"

"He wanted to protect you," Heather realized. "He certainly was mature for his years."

"Yes, he wanted to shield me from the truth as long as possible, but also I think he wanted to live his life as normally as he could. Having me worrying about him would just have made matters worse. But when I learned the truth, I was so terribly angry. I remember when the plane landed, I even felt angry at the world for being so cold and dead and bleak. The sky was gray and somber. We didn't even have any snow to soften the harsh winter scene.

"A professor from the school met us and drove us to the hospital. I didn't even learn his name. It was all like a dream. I couldn't seem to relate to my surroundings. When we pulled up in front of the hospital—all marble and steel and glass—I thought it looked like a mausoleum. Crossing the foyer, a cute little teen-ager in one of those candy-striped uniforms smiled at me. I wondered how anyone could smile. Buddy was dying.

"And then . . .." At last the tears began to well up in her eyes. Too choked to continue, Wanda blinked them back for a few moments. Heather pulled her chair closer to her, offered her a tissue, and squeezed her arm in encouragement.

"I'm sorry," Wanda said unnecessarily. "But I've never told anyone about this before. Somehow it's very difficult to say the words, but I must.

"You see," she continued. "When we stepped off the elevator, we could hear Buddy's screams. He was crying out in torment, in pure agony." The tears finally began to flow.

"He was calling, 'God. O God, please help me! I hurt, God. God, how I hurt!' The doctor came and led us down the hall to his room. Mother went in and stood at the foot of his bed, but I stopped in the doorway. I just didn't have the courage to enter. My brother was lying there. He was tied down to the bed to keep from dislodging the needles and tubes hooked to his body. He didn't seem to recognize us.

"After a few minutes the doctor took us to a small lounge across the hall. 'We can continue keeping him alive, perhaps for as long as a week,' he said. 'But he will remain in the same condition. It would be a week of torment. Or we can let him go.'

"My father looked at my mother, my brave beautiful mother. She knew what he was thinking and nodded her assent. Then—then they looked at me. I was the only one crying. I wanted to scream. To yell. To rebel. I wanted to defy God. To defy the universe. It was so unfair!

"But all I could do was agree. My father told the doctor,

'We'd rather have Buddy spend the next week in glory with his Lord than in agony here with us.'

"The doctor put an understanding hand on his shoulder, then walked resolutely across the hall and pushed open Buddy's door. The three of us huddled together, trying to gain comfort from being near. We had no words to speak.

"In a few minutes the doctor told us we could go in. Buddy was still screaming, writhing in pain, but some of the equipment had been pushed away from his bedside; he was no longer tied down. Mother kept bathing his face with a cold cloth. She tried desperately to do some small thing to comfort him. As the hours wore on, he grew weaker and quieter. At the end, he just seemed to slip into a deep sleep.

"Arrangements were made for the funeral to be held on Monday, Christmas Eve. But I couldn't- — I just couldn't — take another funeral. It was cold, freezing cold, but I went out in the back yard and climbed up into our little tree house and refused to come down.

"My parents wisely decided to let me stay there. From my perch I could see the church's steeple down the street. I knew it would be overflowing with people who loved Buddy and had come to tell him good-bye. But I couldn't. I just couldn't.

"Huddled up in that tree, I realized that I wasn't angry with my parents, or at the world. I was angry at God. He had taken my brothers. I wanted desperately to turn against Him and to claim He didn't exist, but I couldn't even do that. In that tree-top I was so totally aware of His presence. I could almost feel His arms around me — loving me, comforting, understanding my heartache.

"At last I realized how very cold I was. I climbed stiffly down the tree and went into the kitchen and made myself some hot chocolate. Buddy loved hot chocolate with lots of little marshmallows in it. So that's the way I made it. I sat there all alone, sipping the scalding liquid and thinking.

"I thought of how Buddy had lived the past few years. He knew the chances were against him having a normal lifespan. And yet, he had lived those years to the fullest. He laughed and played and enjoyed life. He made plans for the future, just as if he were going to live to be a hundred. I realized he would want me to do the same.

"A few days later I took the bus into Minneapolis to do some research in the big library there. I found a medical textbook on hematology. With the help of a dictionary, I plowed through the pages of information about hemophilia. I saw a chart that showed my chances of being a carrier were 50-50. Then the author advised that the only way the disease could ever be eradicated would be if all those who had any possibility of being a carrier would determine never to marry or risk having children."

"Oh, Wanda! How sad," Heather blurted out as she blew into another tissue. "And you were how old?"

"Eighteen. I vowed to take that advice. I broke up with my steady and have never had a date since."

"Never? That's unreal!" Heather exclaimed.

"No, it was really quite practical in my situation. The problem is, I didn't just shut myself off from boys but from everyone. I went to a girls' college and even refused to have a roommate. I must have been trying to protect myself. You can't be hurt by people who aren't important to you.

"But as I tried to think of Jesus living my insulated life, I realized how very wrong I've been. I've felt self-righteous because I go to church regularly; I read my Bible and pray daily. Yet I've been a hypocrite because I haven't let myself love. I probably chose to work with retarded adults because I could help them without building too close personal relationships."

"What about your parents?"

"My parents—" The tears welled up again. Wanda blew her nose daintily. "Last year, before I moved here, they were both killed in a car wreck. Heather, can you believe I made all the arrangements, attended the funeral and burial, sold the house and business, turned my back on my town and everyone in it, and never shed a tear?

"Isn't that a disgrace?" she asked as she wiped the tears that were now flowing freely. "I was so completely wrapped up in myself that I couldn't even cry. Until this week I never really considered how I might be hurting others. My grand-mother . . .." She had to stop and blow her nose again. "I am the only living grandchild. My grandmother doesn't even know where I am," Wanda cried ashamedly. "And my moth-er's only sister, my father's family. I've been so completely self-centered." She sobbed and shook her head in remorse.

Heather went to Wanda and put her arms around her. She let her cry on her shoulder. "But you can make it all better now," she consoled Wanda and patted her as if she were a child. They cried together a few more moments; then Wanda pulled away.

"I'll be all right now. Thanks so very much, Heather. It wasn't as bad as I thought it would be."

"But you haven't eaten a thing," Heather protested.

"I've had a much deeper need filled. I need to be alone for a little while now. I'm sure you understand. And I have to get myself composed and back on the job before my volunteers think I have deserted them."

"Volunteers?"

"Oh my, yes. We're dependent on them," Wanda explained as she slipped into her coat. "Think you'd be interested?"

"I might. You'll have to tell me more about it sometime."

"OK," Wanda replied. Then she gave Heather a quick hug.

"I'm—I'm going to call my grandmother tonight. Pray for me?"

Heather nodded.

"I'll let you know how it turns out."

Chapter 10

"What was that all about?" Don asked when Heather finally replaced the receiver of the family-room phone. She waltzed across the room and obviously was very pleased about something. Taking the long yellow pad from his hand, she plopped unceremoniously on his lap.

"That was Wanda," she confided as she snuggled up.

"Well, it sounded very buddy-buddy to me. You two have one lunch together; now all of a sudden you're old friends!"

"Yeah." Heather sighed. "She—she's going to visit her grandmother in a couple of weeks."

"And that's supposed to be a big deal?"

"Well, it's a long story. I don't know if she wants me to tell it yet. We were also talking about something else. Monday afternoon I'm going to the Home so she can give me the grand tour. They use quite a few volunteer workers and are always looking for new recruits."

"You think that might be the project you've been looking for?"

"I don't know, but I believe I should be willing to investigate. If those adults have only childlike abilities, maybe I could use some of the same techniques that work with my 4-year-olds. I had a minor revelation this morning that really impressed me. I've been thinking about it all day."

"Just what great thoughts has my scatterbrain been having?" Don teased as he kissed her on her ear.

"I'm serious," she retorted. "Don't be so patronizing!

Sometimes you treat me like a child."

"Sorry about that," he relented. "You certainly don't make me feel like a child. I will have to admit that occasionally some very profound philosophy is conjured up in that curly noggin of yours. What was it today?"

"Well, I was reading Psalm 119 this morning, in one of the modern versions. In the verse about *thy word is a lamp unto my feet*, the word *lamp* was translated to *flashlight*. I could see that *flashlight* would be a modern-day equivalent, but yet it would be so much more powerful than the flickering little flame the psalmist was familiar with. So I got to thinking about how puny that light must have seemed on a dark night and wondering why it would remind him of God's Word.

"Then all of a sudden I got it! He was used to trusting that lamp to show him how to take just his next step. With modern lighting, you know—streetlights, high-powered beams from headlights and stuff—we are accustomed to being able to see way out in front of us all the time. Maybe we need to depend on the Lord for guidance just one step at a time."

"I see your point," Don agreed. "Very good."

"It was especially significant for me because I've been feeling kind of, well, disappointed that I hadn't had some miraculous vision of what I was to do with the rest of my life. I mean, after all, I had decided I was willing to live my life as Jesus would, so why shouldn't I have had some kind of super-natural road map to guide me? But that verse made me realize it takes more faith to follow step by step and trust that the next step would be illuminated at the proper time."

"Yeah." Don nodded. "I like that. And I have to say that I think making friends with Wanda was a step you needed to take. You really had a very poor attitude toward her."

"I sure did! I was very prejudiced toward her."

"Prejudiced?"

"Yeah. Funny, isn't it? I've always prided myself on my attitude toward minority groups; I truly believed I looked at people as individuals. Yet, I was prejudiced against Wanda, and probably others, because of a beautiful face. Was it just jealousy that would make me feel that anyone so lovely to look at couldn't be beautiful underneath?"

"You really don't have anything to be jealous of, funny face," Don protested. "You may not be beautiful in the classic sense, but I think you are absolutely adorable! With a sparkle in your hazel eyes and a flash of your dimples, you can captivate anyone. Especially me!"

"Thanks for the kind words of encouragement," she murmured as she planted a loud smack on his cheek, "but I did have a very bad attitude. Wouldn't it be rather like poetic justice if it turned out that she is the very person to help me find a really fulfilling role for my life?"

"Well, I'm getting a little jealous of Wanda myself," Don declared as his body stiffened.

"You? Why? What do you mean?"

"Well, first you spend over half an hour talking to her while I sit here writing notes to myself. Now she's dominating our whole conversation when you are supposed to be devoting yourself to me!"

"Aha!" she cried. "The green monster rises again! And just what compelling topic would you like to discuss?"

"Well, I was going to ask for suggestions to help me decide what I'm going to discuss at the sales meeting I've called for Monday morning, but that can wait. Let's go to bed instead."

"OK."

"Now what are we going to do?" Timmy whined.

"Yeah, Mom," Tommy joined in, "we'll miss the game!"

"Well, it just won't start," Heather complained. She had ground and ground the motor, but it refused to catch. Another try produced only a hollow click. "We might as well give up; this car isn't going any place today. C'mon back in the house. I'll call Mrs. Lindholm and ask her to take you to the game with Paul."

Moaning and groaning, the twins bewailed their fate as they dragged their hockey equipment from the station wagon. Heather arranged for their transportation and had just returned the receiver to its hook when the instrument rang.

"Heather, this is Kenny. I'm at the hospital. They are getting Sally Ann ready for surgery."

"But—but, it's too early. What happened?"

"Her hand started shaking while she was serving breakfast this morning. Kinda like a muscle spasm, only worse. It didn't last too long, but I was worried and made her call her doctor. He said to get her over here immediately. They checked her out. Her blood pressure has skyrocketed. Pleurisy, the doctor said. They have to take the baby before Sally Ann goes into convulsions and we lose both of them."

"And you're there alone?"

"Yes, one of our neighbors is keeping our girls."

"I'll be there as soon as I can."

"Thanks. I sure could use someone to talk to," Kenny replied with a catch in his throat.

Dashing outside at the sound of a honking horn, Heather quickly explained the situation to her friend as the twins piled into the car.

"The boys can go home with us after the game," Kathryn Lindholm volunteered. "Don't worry about them. You just stay with your friend as long as he needs you."

"Thanks lots, Kathryn. I'll call you later and check on the boys."

102

Back in the house Heather phoned Wanda, briefed her on the events, and explained her predicament. "I automatically promised to go be with him and forgot that my car won't start. Could you drive me?"

"To the hospital?" Wanda hesitated. "I haven't been inside a hospital since, since Buddy—"

"Oh, I'm sorry, Wanda. I didn't think. That's all right; I'll get someone else."

"No. No, I want to help. Even if I can't get up enough courage to go in, I can at least give you a ride. I'll be there in a few minutes."

The next call was to Don. "But it will be nearly an hour before I get there," Heather concluded. "I realize how busy Saturdays are, but is there any way you could—"

"Sure there is," Don interrupted, rising from his chair. "I'll just leave. The next hour is going to be tough enough on him. I'm sure not going to let him spend it alone. I can get to the hospital in five minutes. See you there."

After a brief explanation, Don turned the customers sitting in his office over to one of his salesmen. "Kenny Campbell, huh?" the fleshy car buyer commented. "Well, I've been a Sox fan for years. You go right ahead. Tell him I hope everything comes out all right."

When Don entered the sixth-floor maternity waiting room, he found Kenny staring vacantly out the window. "You OK, pal?" he asked as he slipped a companionable arm over the ballplayer's shoulders.

"Don?" Kenny asked. He first looked surprised, then puzzled, and then pleased. "Hey, man, it's sure good of you to take off and come over here."

"No big deal. Heard any more about Sally Ann?"

"They just wheeled her into the operating room. I got to talk to her a minute. She looked so young." Kenny stopped, shook his head, then cleared his throat. "So very young and beautiful.

"And you know what, Don? All she talked about was the baby. She sounded kinda fuzzy and dopey; she didn't really make sense, but her only thought was for the baby. Didn't seem concerned about herself at all. But I sure am!" He sighed.

Kenny shuffled across the room and sank into one of the blue-green plastic chairs. Slouching down and stretching his long legs, he contemplated his sneakered feet while he twisted the plain gold wedding band on his left hand.

"Don," he asked at last, "can someone trust the Lord and be scared at the same time?"

"You wouldn't be human if you weren't a little apprehensive in a situation like this, but I'm sure the Lord will give you peace no matter what happens. I also think this little cubbyhole of a waiting room was made to drive people stir-crazy. Let's go down to the cafeteria and get a cup of coffee. We won't have any news for a while yet. Some coffee will help the time pass."

They lingered over their coffee as long as possible and then stopped by the gift shop, where Kenny ordered flowers for his wife and Don bought a newspaper. Then they returned to the small waiting room.

Shortly before 11:30, Heather, her hair windblown and cheeks rosy from the cold, hurried down the corridor toward the waiting area. Wanda followed a few steps behind; she looked rather pale and subdued.

"Have you heard anything yet?" Heather asked as she greeted Kenny and Don.

"No," Kenny replied anxiously, "but it shouldn't be too much longer."

"I'd have been here sooner, but my car wouldn't start," she

explained with a tumble of words that displayed her nervousness. "I think it's the battery, Don. So Wanda brought me; we nearly froze because her heater didn't get fixed right. Don't you have any pull with your mechanics at all?" She sounded so indignant that Kenny smiled and momentarily forgot his own problems.

"Do you get this kind of static all the time, Don?" he asked.

"Yeah, you sell a car. Then people take it as a personal insult anytime they have trouble with it. But never fear; I shall take care of your little problems, madam. Especially that heater." He scowled. "You shouldn't have had any more trouble with that."

"I'm sorry about your difficulties," Kenny said more seriously, "and I appreciate your wanting to be here. Both of you. It helps to have friends who care."

"I feel rather useless," Wanda muttered. Then she added very intently, "but I do care."

"Thanks."

"What about your daughters? Would you like me to keep them while Sally Ann is in the hospital?" Heather asked.

"Oh, no thanks. I called my mother-in-law as soon as I brought Sally Ann in. She is flying here to care for them. I'm going to have to meet her at the airport this afternoon, too," Kenny remembered. He rummaged in his shirt pocket and pulled out a slip of paper that in large, blue numerals had the flight number and time of arrival written on it.

"Let me have that," Heather demanded. She pulled the paper from his hands. "I'll find someone to meet her so you don't have to leave. What does Sally Ann's mother look like?"

"Well, she's a small woman. You'll see a strong family resemblance; anyone who knows Sally Ann would probably recognize her. She'll likely be wearing a new grey coat we bought her for Christmas. And she'll have a bewildered expression. This'll be her first experience at O'Hare. I hate to be a bother to anyone, though."

"Not another word. You're needed here," Heather insisted as she started for the phone booth down the hall. A few minutes later she returned with a triumphant expression. "Jan and Al are going to pick her up; they were glad to be able to do something helpful."

Wanda began pacing back and forth in the small room. "Why do they make all hospital waiting rooms look exactly the same?" she asked rhetorically. "Heather, maybe you could start a campaign to redecorate these torture chambers."

Just then a tall sandy-haired man in a faded green scrub suit entered.

"Dr. Davis!" Kenny exclaimed, jumping to his feet. "How is she?"

"She's out of danger; she'll be fine."

"Oh, wow!" Kenny responded exuberantly with relief splashed across his face. "Praise the Lord! Can I see her?"

"Not yet; she's still in recovery. I'd suggest you go have some lunch and give her time to wake up a bit. Now about your son—"

"My son," Kenny repeated, a little stunned.

"Yes, he's a little small—less than five pounds—but perfectly developed. His sudden entry into the world was quite a shock to his system, though. He's having a little problem breathing. I called in one of the best pediatricians in the field. He's been with him since birth. If anyone can pull him through, it's Dr. Pittman."

"Dr. Pittman? Josh? I can't think of anyone I'd rather have."

"Oh, you know each other. Well, that explains why Jackie is with him. Your son is in good hands. I have an office full of patients to see, but I'll be back to check Sally Ann later. See you then," the obstetrician promised.

"How about that? I have a son!" Kenny announced as much to himself as to his three smiling companions. "You all might not believe this, but I was so concerned about Sally Ann that I had forgotten all about the baby. A boy! I wonder if Sally Ann knows. Sure hope the little fellow is all right."

After a quick lunch the four friends returned to find a white-clad Jackie waiting impatiently for them. Her lips formed a faint smile of greeting, but the look of concern never left her round, black eyes.

"Kenny, what's the baby's name?" she asked softly.

"His name? Why, it's Wade. Wade Campbell. That's Sally Ann's maiden name. How is he?"

"He's having trouble breathing, Kenny, but he's a spunky little guy and he's fighting."

"When—how long before you'll know if he'll make it?"

"The first 72 hours are the most critical. We'll keep you informed," she assured him. Then she returned to the preemie nursery.

A few minutes later Sally Ann was wheeled into her room a short distance down the hall. Kenny was allowed to join her.

"How much longer do you think we should hang around here?" Don questioned restlessly. "I'm willing to stay as long as needed, but with Kenny at his wife's bedside, how valuable is our presence?"

"Well, the Bonnells should be arriving soon with Sally Ann's mother," Heather said. "Let's wait until they get here. Just in case . . .."

"Good suggestion," Don agreed. "Think I'll call the office while I'm waiting."

"Heather, Don, and Wanda were all relieved when Jan and Al arrived a half-hour later with the surprisingly young-appearing Mrs. Wade. While the six of them were becoming acquainted, no one noticed as Josh Pittman passed the waiting-room door on his way to talk with the Campbells. He retraced his steps a few minutes later and stopped to be introduced to Mrs. Wade.

To the anxious inquiries about the baby's condition, he replied, "He's doing about as well as can be expected, under the circumstances. I just came from Sally Ann's room. She requested that everyone pray for the baby. We don't generally allow visitors this soon after surgery, but I think we could bend the rules enough to permit a short prayer session. You may all go quietly to her room; I'll get Jackie and we'll join you."

When everyone had tiptoed into position around the hospital bed, a reverent hush fell over them. Kenny was holding Sally Ann's right hand. Automatically the others joined hands and formed a circle around the bed. As they bowed their heads, a surge of power like a current of electricity flowed through the group. Each of them was acutely aware of another Presence in the room.

As Kenny began a faltering, hesitant prayer, they were enveloped by an overcompassing power of concentrated love that banded them together as never before. Their anxious prayers of petition turned to pronouncements of praise as the austere hospital room was transformed to a cathedral of joy.

"Wade's going to be all right," Sally Ann proclaimed when the prayers had ended. "I have a deep assurance of it now. Our son is going to live!"

Chapter 11

On Sunday morning as they were preparing to leave for Sunday school, Heather and Don were still discussing the experience at the hospital.

"I'm afraid the worship services this morning are going to be anticlimactic," Heather concluded as she gathered up the supplies for the handwork project she had planned for her class. Then, as they were walking out the door, the phone rang.

A shiver of apprehension ran down Heather's spine as she handed Don her armload of supplies and hurried to the phone. To her great relief it was just one of her teacher helpers who apologetically canceled out at the last minute.

"Well, you'll just have to come and help," she informed Don. "I don't have time to find anyone else."

"Me?" he recoiled. "I'd feel silly in a class of 4-year-olds!"

"Oh, my goodness. Your dignity won't be ruffled, and they love to have daddies visit the class. Besides, remember what Kenny said about couples working together?"

"Rumble—rumble," he growled in his best Fred Flintstone imitation. "I have the feeling I'm being railroaded." The twins laughed with glee at the thought of their father having to serve in the beginner's department.

To Don's great surprise he soon found himself enjoying the youngsters. He took off his suit coat and tie, rolled up his sleeves, and plunged into the gooey process of making heart-shaped Valentine tiles to be given to the children's parents next week.

He watched in awe as the 27 beginners clustered around Heather in a semicircle for story time. The upturned faces were completely captivated by the puppets' version of the good Samaritan. He had known for years how much Heather enjoyed her class, but he had never realized how very good she was with the children. Even without formal training as an educator, Heather clearly had a natural aptitude.

As they walked toward the sanctuary later, he grudgingly admitted, "That was fun. I'd forgotten how cute they are at that age. And after seeing how competently you handle those kids, I think you might be a real assist at the Home."

Those words of encouragement inspired Heather as she flew through her Monday marathon cleanup. Even though she felt a little guilty about not doing quite as thorough a job as usual, precisely at 2 she bounded up the broad, low, concrete steps of the Home. Through the glass door she could see Wanda walking toward her and smiling.

"Glad to see you, Heather," was Wanda's warm greeting. "And right on time, too. Have you heard from Kenny today?" she asked as they crossed the rectangular reception foyer toward the open door of her office.

"Talked to him a few minutes this morning. He says both Sally Ann and Wade sleep most of the time, which I guess is good."

Heather glanced around the paneled office at the brightly colored pictures and the array of plants that gave the room a cheerful appearance as Wanda hung her coat on a clothes tree in the corner. The friendly atmosphere made Heather feel more comfortable.

"I hate to expose my ignorance," she began with a grimace, "but I know next to nothing about the Home. You'll have to fill me in."

"What would you like to know?"

"Well, mostly about your, uh, people. Just how retarded are they?"

"We don't like to use the word *retarded*," Wanda explained. "They are classified as neurologically handicapped. The handicaps differ according to which lobe of the brain has been damaged."

"Oh. What causes this damage?"

"Different things. Genetic defects, prenatal German measles, and brain damage during birth are what account for many of the difficulties. Then some were born normal but suffered damage because of accidents, falls, spinal meningitis, measles, mastoid infections, and various other reasons. Perhaps the saddest cases are those with a disease that causes brain deterioration, because they become progressively worse."

"Oh, that must be tough to watch," Heather empathized.

"Yes, it is. And not everyone is emotionally equipped for this kind of work," Wanda warned softly.

"Well, I thought I might be able to use some of the same games and projects that work with my 4-year-olds.

"Some of them might be adaptable."

"And perhaps I could bring my puppets and have them tell stories."

"I'm sure they'd enjoy that, but you must remember they learn very slowly, if at all. It sometimes takes infinite patience to teach the most elementary things."

"For example?"

"Well, about a year ago we enrolled one 35-year-old woman who hadn't been toilet-trained. Personally, I don't think anyone ever bothered to try, but it was well worth the effort."

"I believe it," Heather responded as she curled up her nose.

"I don't think I'd like that task. That was the most distasteful thing about rearing the twins."

"Oh, but we didn't do it just for our convenience," Wanda exclaimed. "This was a great personal accomplishment to her. It's amazing how much self-respect and self-confidence she has gained. She likes herself more. I think that is very important!"

"Oh, of course. I didn't think of it that way," Heather replied contritely.

"C'mon, let's go look around," Wanda suggested as she led the way across the foyer and down the wide hall that divided the building in two.

"I must caution you, Heather, to use some discretion about the questions you ask in front of these pupils. You wouldn't want to upset them. Mondays are bad enough."

"Mondays?"

"Yes, our residents are chronologically adults, but they still react to any upset in their schedules just as small children do. Weekends always seem to get them keyed up—more excitable and less manageable, especially if they have had visitors."

"Yes, now that I think of it, the twins reacted that way when they were little. Oh, what's all this?" Heather asked. She stopped in front of a long, lighted case full of trophies and ribbons.

"Awards our people have won in the Special Olympics and other contests," Wanda beamed. "You'd be surprised how well-coordinated some of them are. They have a lot of fun since they are competing against their peers. See the bowling trophies? The alley on Route 58, just north of here, allows us to use its facilities once a week. We don't rack up very high scores, but we have a good time. And it's good to get away from the Home occasionally.

"We take them on many such trips—to professional ball

games, concerts, museums, and things like that. We usually take them only once a week; it's something geared to their individual interests. Not everyone goes to everything; of course, these outings require more volunteers."

"That would be something I could do. Don might even be able to go along sometimes."

"Uh-huh," Wanda murmured noncommitedly. "Now, this is an observation room," she explained as she opened the door to what looked like a long, poorly lighted hall. "This window is a mirror on the other side, so we can observe without being seen. A great deal can be learned through what I call 'creative play,' especially when they don't know they're being watched."

Heather peered through the window at the large, well-lighted room which seemed full of activity. In the corner to her right a gray-haired woman was rocking a rag doll. She paid little attention to the platinum-haired young woman talking to her.

"How old is that woman?" Heather inquired softly.

"She's in her early 50s. She's one of our long-time residents; she's been here more than 20 years. That doll is her security symbol. We feel no necessity for weaning her from it. She needs a sense of security."

"She doesn't seem to be listening to anything the volunteer is telling her."

"Volunteer?" Wanda questioned. "Oh, you mean Sunny. She isn't a volunteer; she is our newest resident."

"You mean that beautiful young girl is—is—" Heather was too shocked to continue.

"Yes," Wanda replied gently. "She suffered brain damage during what must have been a very difficult labor. Her mother died; until recently she was reared by her grandparents. They called her 'Sunny' because of her delightful disposition. She always seems happy and bubbly."

"How—how bad is her, uh, handicap?"

"She checked out about early 3-year-old level, but I think she has improved already. For one thing, until she arrived here, she had no playmates. She really seems to enjoy being around people. She's very enthusiastic about the equipment here, especially the playground. She is quite well-coordinated; she'll probably do well in the next Olympics."

"She looks happy. What is the man doing in the big sand-box?"

"That's John. He has the mentality of about a 2 1/2- or 3-year-old, but he has an amazingly long attention span. He will work literally hours at creating a whole town in that box. He'll make hills and valleys, winding roads, and a busy downtown section. He uses different-sized blocks to represent houses and buildings. Toy cars run up and down the streets. Some of the towns are creative masterpieces, but when he finishes, he always destroys them."

"Why?"

"I'm not sure. He had some very sad experiences before he joined us here. Unlike Sunny, who was given love and security by her grandparents, he was shifted from one bad situation to another. He could sense he was not wanted and never knew when he would be sent away.

"We try to make them feel they belong here and give them a sense of permanency. And affection. We've found, Heather, that even the most severely handicapped people respond to love. Shall we go meet some of them?"

They left the observation room and entered another door which led to the middle of the playroom. Heather wandered over to a table where a middle-aged man was winding black cord in and out and around nails he had placed on a yellow board.

"Why, he's making a design!" she exclaimed.

The man turned big brown eyes to her and smiled.

"I'll say he is," Wanda agreed. "Paul makes beautiful pictures with his string. He creates some really intricate designs. No two of them are the same. We're quite proud of him," Wanda exclaimed with an affectionate pat on his back. Paul beamed and returned to his work.

"I'll bet he could sell some of those," Heather commented as they walked away.

"I'm sure he could, but he won't part with any. He has a solid wall of them in his room. I don't know what we'll do when he runs out of wall space, because he refuses to even hang them in the hall outside his room.

"Now, I'd like you to meet Sunny. Sunny, this is my friend, Heather," Wanda explained to the bright-eyed 20-year-old.

"Will you be my friend, too?" Sunny asked.

"I'd like that." Heather smiled.

"Would you read me a story?"

Heather looked questioningly at Wanda, who nodded approval.

"I certainly will, Sunny. What book shall I read?"

Sunny grabbed Heather by the hand and pulled her toward the long bookcase built under the windows as Wanda crossed to the other side of the room to talk to one of the volunteers.

"Read this," Sunny demanded as she handed Heather a well-worn copy of *The Three Little Pigs*. Heather sat in the nearest chair, opened the book, and began to read.

"I like the snow," Sunny announced suddenly as she looked out the window. "I like the grass, too. When we have grass, leaves grow on the trees."

"Don't you want me to read to you?" Heather asked.

"When the leaves grow, the birds come and sing. Do you like birds? I like birds. They sing to me. I think I'll go rock my doll some more," Sunny declared and wandered back to the corner of the room that was set up like a living room.

A very nonplussed Heather sat holding the open book. She did not know whether she should follow Sunny or not.

Wanda observed her perplexity and walked across the room. "Would you like to see some of the handcraft projects in the workroom?"

Heather nodded and replaced the little book on the shelf. As they walked toward the door, a short, black-haired woman walked up to Wanda. The woman had a wooden puzzle in her hands.

"Look what I did, Wanda!" she announced proudly.

"Why, Edna Jean! Did you really work that puzzle all by yourself?" Wanda asked with wonderment. Edna Jean nodded. "Well, that is a real accomplishment! This is one of the hardest puzzles we have," Wanda explained to Heather.

"When Edna Jean arrived here six months ago, she was clutching a coloring book and crayons; those were the only toys she had to play with. Now she is learning so many new things! She is even beginning to read, aren't you?"

Wanda placed an arm around the shorter woman and gave her a friendly hug. "I'm very pleased that you can work that puzzle. After my friend leaves, I'll come back and watch you. Right now I'm going to take her to the workshop and show her the potholders you made. All right?"

Edna Jean shyly nodded her approval and returned to the table, where she dumped out the puzzle pieces to begin over again.

"Will she really be able to learn to read?" Heather asked when they were safely in the hall.

"She'll never manage *War and Peace,* but she'll master easy readers. Most of all, she is so pleased with herself that it is a delight to see."

"What—what is her story?"

"She has been shifted around by various relatives. Before coming here she stayed with an aunt who kept her locked in her apartment for nearly two years. There wasn't even a balcony so she could get fresh air. Can you imagine being incarcerated like that?"

"Why on earth was her aunt so cruel?"

"Because Edna Jean has had two illegitimate babies. She was just trying to protect her."

"But what about her children?"

"Edna Jean doesn't even remember them. If you ask her about her pregnancies, she'll tell you that she used to be fat."

"But who? What kind of man would take advantage of such a woman?"

"I've asked myself the same question. It's pathetic, but you can see that these people do need to be protected from some of the realities of life."

"Yes," Heather agreed. She was visibly shaken by her experiences in the playroom.

"Are you all right?" Wanda inquired. "You look rather pale."

"I'm fine," Heather insisted. "Let's continue."

They entered a room of identical size; it contained six long worktables with four to six adults working at each table. As they walked along, Heather observed handcrafts ranging from simple paste-and-glue projects to intricate leather-tooling. Wanda pointed out two brightly colored potholders Edna Jean had looped. She also was making a wastebasket fashioned from empty egg cartons.

Without pausing to introduce her visitor to anyone, Wanda led her back into the hall. "Was that easier?" she asked.

"Yes, but . . . but . . . Wanda, do you realize I can't tell who is—is a volunteer and who isn't?" Heather quivered.

"With your inexperienced eye, I'm sure you couldn't. Do you want to continue?"

"Yes," Heather declared determinedly as she bit her lower lip.

They crossed the hall and entered a huge indoor playground that was twice the size of the other rooms.

"Isn't this fantastic?" Wanda asked. "This room, our gym, and the indoor pool were gifts of a wealthy family whose son has been in the Home nearly 25 years."

"Oh, this is great. I'll bet they all enjoy this," Heather commented as she watched the men and women swinging on the oversized gym sets and going down the slide.

"The ones who are able do. You haven't seen any of our severely handicapped people."

"You mean some of them are so severely handicapped they can't even play?"

"Oh my, yes. But they all respond to love, Heather. They all have needs. Why, we have one young man who is bedridden—he can't even sit up—and is totally blind. Yet he recognizes his parents when they visit. He smiles for them. For more than 15 years they have driven 600 miles each month to see their son smile."

"Oh, stop," Heather pleaded. "Don't tell me any more. I just can't take it," she admitted as tears began welling in her eyes.

"Oh, yes you can," Wanda snapped. "You are not to lose control in here and upset these people." The sharpness of her words shocked Heather so much that she blinked and regained her composure.

After they returned to the hall, Wanda said softly, "If you can make it to my office, I'll take my turn to share some tissues."

Heather nodded with a sniffle; the two hurried to the privacy of Wanda's room. Then Heather dissolved into tears as she plopped down on the leather couch. "I'm so sorry," she cried, as she accepted the much-needed tissues. "I was so happy and excited about volunteering. I thought maybe I could be useful here, but just look at me! I can't even control my emotions. I feel so foolish!"

"Don't blame yourself," Wanda advised. "I tried to warn you that not everyone is suited to this kind of work. It takes a rather stoic personality, which is why I'd never mentioned the need of volunteers to you. If you recall, you are the one who asked me about it."

"Yes, I know. I was so enthusiastic, and now I feel guilty because I just can't hack it."

"Oh, please don't! You'll give me a complex, too," Wanda protested. "I shouldn't have let you visit when I had reservations about you being able to deal with it."

"Oh, it isn't your fault! I insisted," Heather acknowledged as she quieted down. "But I feel so useless, Wanda. I'm not good at anything."

"That's not true! It's the very warmth of your personality and your ability to empathize with others that make working with these people impossible. But that same trait is the one which makes you such a good friend and confidante. People respond to you because you care. Don't underestimate yourself, Heather."

"But what can I do? I like people and try to be friendly, but I'm just not a joiner. Garden clubs and bridge parties bore me silly. I realize I am entirely too devoted to my home. Jesus wouldn't lavish so much affection on a house, but what can I do with my time that would be productive?"

"I'm afraid I can't answer that."

"I feel like going home and eating everything in the house that isn't nailed down!"

"In other words, you're frustrated."

"Yes, that's it exactly. I'm not really hungry! I'm just frustrated. I wonder how often that's true?"

"Well, now that you realize that isn't the solution, what are you going to do?"

"I'll just have to wait for some more light," Heather decided.

"More light?"

"It's a little 'in' thing between me and the Lord," Heather explained as she patted her cheeks dry. She rose from the couch and threw the soggy tissues in the large green basket.

Chapter 12

Heather fed the boys on schedule that evening but waited to eat with Don so they could talk. The clock showed nearly 8 when he appeared with a big grin and a kiss.

"And how was your day today?" he asked as he mimicked the question she habitually greeted him with.

"Well, I don't think I'll be signing on as a volunteer," she replied noncommittally. "How did your sales meeting go?"

"Better and worse than I expected," he replied as they sat down to eat. He held her hand and prayed and then continued the conversation. "On the way to work I was going over in my mind all the items listed on my outline you had helped me with. I wanted to be certain to cover every possible way a customer could be taken advantage of. I was so concerned that I might forget something; then suddenly it dawned on me. It's impossible to think of every contingency, and yet Jesus covered it all in the Golden Rule."

"Well, of course," Heather agreed. Her fork stopped in midair. "Why didn't we think of that before? It's so obvious!"

"Yeah, now it is. So instead of the big long speech and the list of do's and don'ts I had prepared, I just had a friendly talk with the staff. I told our employees that in all our dealings with the public I wanted the Golden Rule to be our standard. I said I was very sincere about it and that I intended to enforce it."

"And what was the reaction?"

"Some seemed to think it was a big joke. Sam and William

know me well enough that they understood, but naturally our comedians had to ham it up. Hal started teasing and said the next thing they know I'd be doing my own TV commercials."

"In other words, he thought the idea was corny!"

"Yeah, but you have to admit he is a witty character. He even suggested that I call myself 'Ford's Golden Ruler.'"

"Good pun." Heather chuckled.

"But he didn't think it was so funny when he discovered I was in earnest. After a lengthy discussion he let it be known that he's going to be looking around for employment elsewhere. A couple of others may follow suit. They all seem to think I'm going to lose my shirt."

He leaned forward and looked Heather straight in the eyes. "What if I do, hon? If sticking with this thing really means losing money, are you with me?"

"Of course," she insisted. "We don't need so much money anyway. We don't have any debts; we could cut down our expenses if necessary. But I just don't believe you will lose business in the long run. Maybe I'm too naive."

"Well, they are concerned because every time there is any sort of national monetary crisis, the automobile industry is the first hit. They feel we need to cushion our sales a little more than I outlined. Well, we'll see.

"Do you want to tell me about your tour of the Home? I know you're disappointed, so if you don't want to talk about it yet, I'll understand."

"Now, how do you know that?" Heather wondered. "Did you talk to Wanda?"

"Oh, my dear, sweet funny face," Don laughed as he spooned sugar into his coffee. He stirred the sweet liquid, took a sip, and then explained. "Your every emotion is written clearly on your face for all the world to see. Besides, if you had been enthusiastic about the visit, I never would have gotten a word in edgewise."

"*Humph*, you just know me too well! I was rather relieved you didn't ask too many questions when you came in, 'cause I'm not ready to talk about it. I'm not as downhearted as I was at first. Something else will turn up. Who knows, I might wind up having to help you mind the store!"

"You might at that," Don agreed goodnaturedly.

While she was ironing the next morning, Heather thought about the psalm she had read earlier. She had found no message—no particular insight to encourage her. *Maybe I'm just not reading in the right place,* she thought discontentedly. *Or am I expecting too much? Perhaps if I read some of the teachings of Jesus. Now why didn't I think of that sooner? Surely the most obvious way to know how to live as Jesus would is to read what He taught His followers.*

Leaving Don's half-ironed shirt hanging limply over the ironing board, she pulled the iron plug and hurried to her Bible. Curling up in the big black chair, she began reading the fifth chapter of Matthew.

Nothing in the Beatitudes seemed to fit her; she wasn't poor or hungry or persecuted. She skimmed through Jesus' interpretations of various Jewish laws, but none of them applied to her. She continued into the sixth chapter. Christ's admonition against appearing to be pious to impress others made her stop and reevaluate her motives. "No," she concluded, "I don't want anyone to think I'm great; I just want to help others as Jesus did." She continued her reading.

"Now that's it!" she said excitedly as she reached Matthew 7:7. "'*Ask, and it shall be given to you; seek, and ye shall find; knock, and it shall be opened unto you.*' That's it; that's the verse I'm going to claim, Lord. You know I have asked. I certainly have been seeking. My motives are unselfish. I believe

I'm willing to do whatever You want me to. Please, Lord, open the door for me."

Visit Teresa and her grandmother.

"Teresa? Who's Teresa, and why did I think of that? Oh, yes, that's the little girl Josh told us about. But they speak Spanish, and my Spanish is so rusty I doubt if I could communicate."

VISIT TERESA AND HER GRANDMOTHER.

"I'd certainly feel foolish going to someone's home when I couldn't talk to them, Lord, but if You want me to try, I will. I know. I'll call Josh for the address. If You don't want me to go, then someway or other, make it impossible for me to find them. OK?"

Elena Garcia had been up well before dawn cooking a substantial breakfast for her husband, her two grown sons, and her husband's nephew who was living with them. The men worked diligently on the dairy farm where they lived. Elena took pride in feeding them well.

The three rooms they shared in half-a-frame duplex were small, but Elena found them adequate. They had a private bath, hot and cold running water, and the house was warm and snug despite the coldest winter wind.

When Elena finished wiping the last of the breakfast dishes, she placed the bowl on the shelf above the sink. Hanging her damp drying towel on its nail, she turned to her tiny granddaughter who still sat staring at the oatmeal in her dish.

"My precious little one," she clucked in Spanish, "what will become of you if you don't eat? Well, sitting there any longer won't help. Come, you can help Grandma make the beds."

She swung Teresa down to the floor and went to make her sons' double bed that occupied one corner of the living room.

Teresa slowly followed as far as the doorway, then stood and watched, chewing on the end of one of her long black curls. When her grandmother entered the bedroom, Teresa followed to that doorway and observed the repeat performance with her grandparents' bed. Then the grandmother paused in front of the baby crib that her husband had made safe and sturdy with bailing wire.

"No!" Teresa shrieked shrilly, running toward her prized possession.

"Only one word you know," her grandmother remonstrated, "and you must say it so loudly!" She returned to the living room, where she carefully folded the blankets her nephew had left on the couch and then placed them out of sight under her sons' bed. Returning to the kitchen for her broom, she heard a familiar knock on the door that connected the two kitchens of the duplex.

The gentle face of her young neighbor appeared in the half-opened doorway. "I have a cup of coffee for you, if you have time," was the welcome invitation.

"Thank you, Rosita. You know I enjoy the company as much as the coffee," the older woman accepted graciously.

"Teresa, would you like to come visit me, too?" Rosita asked the somber child. "My boys would love to play with you. They would share their toys." Teresa merely turned her back.

"We'll leave the door open for you," her grandmother said softly. "We would be very happy to have you with us."

With a deep sigh, Elena sat down at her neighbor's table. "I wish I knew what was wrong with the child. I would do anything I could to help her. Each night I ask the good God to show me how."

"Listen," Rosita interrupted. A knock resounded on the Garcias' front door.

"Who could that be?" Elena wondered. "My family never knocks." Hesitantly she returned to her half of the bungalow and made her way to the front door.

"Senora Garcia?" a friendly looking woman asked when Elena opened the door a crack.

Elena nodded affirmatively.

"I am Heather Novak. I'm a friend of Dr. Joshua Pittman from the Holy Name Hospital," she explained in halting Spanish.

"Ah, yes! Come in," Elena invited, opening the door wide. "Any friend of the kind doctor is my friend, too. Do come in," she repeated warmly. "My house is your house!"

"Thank you," Heather replied hesitantly. "I must apologize for my Spanish. I studied many years ago, or, ago many years I studied," she repeated as she corrected her sentence structure.

"You do fine," Elena said. She encouraged her with a big smile. "Come, have a cup of coffee with my neighbor and me," she invited slowly.

"Thank you. You are very kind," Heather replied. She was surprised to find the correct phrase slipping off her tongue. "Dr. Pittman told me, perhaps, you would like help to change the bandage. For Teresa. I brought some things," she explained as best she could. Heather indicated a brown paper bag she held in her arm.

"Already this morning I changed the bandage," Elena replied. "But come. Meet Teresa." She walked over to the child who had been the silent observer of the scene. Picking her up, she said to Teresa, "This kind lady is—how do you pronounce your name again?"

"Novak. Heather Novak. Please call me *Heather*."

"Heather," Elena attempted.

"Yes, Heather. It is difficult in Spanish," she said.

"But it is a beautiful name," Elena declared. She tried it

couple more times. "It sounds like a soft, gentle breeze."

"My, how poetic," Heather responded. "Teresa, can you say my name?"

"She doesn't talk any more," Elena explained sadly. "But come, let us have our coffee."

Heather followed her hostess into the neighbor's kitchen, where she met Rosita and her three noisy sons. When Elena explained her presence to Rosita, Heather realized how very slowly she had been speaking for her benefit. She could understand very little of the rapid flow of words. The three boys soon lost their shyness and began talking to her. The musical flow of Spanish words seemed to envelop her. She felt a little bewildered.

"I am sorry," Elena apologized. "We are talking too rapidly."

"No, you don't talk too rapidly; I listen too slowly," Heather replied. The boys especially thought this was hilarious and joined gleefully in the laughter. Heather's ability to laugh at herself put the others at ease. The three women were soon chatting away.

Haltingly, Heather told of the honeymoon trip she and Don had taken through Mexico. While she extolled the beauties of Mexico and the friendliness of the people she had met, Heather kept stopping to correct her grammar until finally she confessed, "My mouth works faster than my brain!"

Amid polite protests, she declared, "I wish I learned, I had learned, Spanish as a child. Children learn languages so much easier."

"I hope so," Rosita exclaimed. "Next year my two oldest sons will have to start kindergarten.

"Oh, are they twins?"

"No, I held Guillermo back a year so they could start together. I thought it would be easier for them."

"They seem like very sharp boys. I'll bet they could learn quickly. Would you like to play a game with me?" Heather asked. They responded with great enthusiasm.

"I'll tell you English names and you tell me Spanish. OK? Stove," she said, placing her hand on the large white object.

"*Hornillo*," all three boys responded gleefully.

"Salt and pepper," she announced, holding up the objects.

"*Sal y pimienta*."

"Sink."

"*Fregadero*."

"Shelf."

"*Estante*."

"Wall."

"*Pared*."

Then Heather reviewed the words. To her great chagrin, and the boys' delight, she remembered only three of the Spanish words and they remembered all the English. She tried another set of six words. Again she remembered only half while they retained them all. Jumping back to the original words, she forgot one she had right the first time. They remembered all the English.

"Oh, how frustrating!" she said in English as she laughed. She lacked the words to express her emotions in Spanish. She smiled at the boys who were enjoying themselves immensely. Then she turned to the two huge black eyes that had been watching from the doorway.

"Would you like to play, too, Teresa?" she asked. The youngster ducked out of sight.

"What shall I do with her?" the grandmother exclaimed. "I do not know. Each time I pray I ask, but still I do not know. I believe you are a friend," she told Heather as she placed a work-worn hand on her arm. "Can you tell me? Is the child crazy or stupid or what?"

"Oh, I wouldn't know," Heather replied. "I'm certainly no expert, but it seemed to me she understood exactly what we were doing in that game. I do have a friend who might be able to help. If you would like, I'll ask whether she could visit here and examine Teresa. If she can't help, I'm sure she would know who could."

"Oh, yes, please. Bring anyone who might help. I love the child so much. Bring your friend after lunch. I must cook lunch for my men, but after that, please, bring your friend."

"I don't know if she will be able to visit here today," Heather hesitated. She did not want to hurt the anxious woman. "I'll go ask her. I'll stop by this afternoon and tell you what she says."

As Heather rose to leave, both women told her how much they had enjoyed her visit. Heather wished she had the words to express how very glad she was she had come.

"I'll be back after a while to tell you what my friend says," she promised as she stepped out into the cold winter wind.

"Yes, I remember Josh mentioning Teresa," Wanda replied when Heather called and told her of her morning's adventure. "If the child had had any physical reason for her withdrawal, I'm sure he would have found it. If she has normal intelligence, I could tell in a few minutes, but if not, it might take some intensive testing."

"Would you go with me and check her out? It would mean a great deal to her grandmother."

"Sure. I could go this afternoon from 2 to 3. I usually allot that time for appointments, but I'm free today. Since it's near-by—"

"I'll be there at 2 o'clock to pick you up," Heather promised.

When the two friends arrived at the Garcias' home, Wanda

asked to be left alone with Teresa, so Heather and Elena went to visit Rosita, who was naturally curious about what was happening.

Wanda pulled a flat, yellow board from the bag she was carrying and placed it beside her on the faded couch. Teresa stood in the doorway; the child watched but displayed no great interest. Then Wanda dug into the bag to find six different-colored disks which were shaped to fit into the depressions on the board.

First she took the round, red disk and tried to fit it in one after another of the slots. When it finally slipped into the round hole, she gave a sigh of satisfaction but did not turn to see Teresa's reaction. She repeated the procedure with each of the disks. By this time Teresa had inched closer so she could see what this strange, pale lady was doing.

Wanda turned the board over. She dumped the disks out on the couch and purposely allowed a couple of the pieces to fall to the floor. Again she went through the routine of finding the correct position for each of the shapes. She then looked under the board and all around the couch "searching" for the missing pieces. At last Teresa picked up the yellow triangle that lay at her feet and handed it to Wanda.

"No!" Teresa called out as Wanda attempted to force the triangle into the square hole. She pushed Wanda's hand to the proper place and then picked up the green square and positioned it.

Wanda had to use all her discipline not to smile. She calmly turned over the board again and then turned her attention to her bag while she watched Teresa from the corner of her eye. The child picked up the pieces and on the first try placed each in the correct spot. Then she looked boldly at Wanda with a smug look of self-satisfaction.

"Nothing's wrong with you," Wanda whispered with a

pleased smile. "You're a real sharpie! Would you like to play with these for a while?" Wanda asked as she poured several plastic blocks from her bag. Teresa gave them a disdainful look. Then she turned over the board and spilled the pieces again.

"OK, you can play with that; I'm going to talk to your grandmother," Wanda told her, even though she doubted that the child understood.

Elena held her breath when Wanda walked through the kitchen door. "She's very smart," Wanda reported.

"*Es muy lista!*" Heather translated happily.

"Thanks to God!" Elena exclaimed.

Amid many smiles Wanda was given a seat and introduced to Rosita. "I can't help but wonder though," Wanda told Heather. "If there is no physical or mental problem, there must have been some kind of emotional shock. Could you ask Mrs. Garcia?"

"I haven't the vaguest idea how to say emotional shock," Heather moaned. "Just a minute. I'll look it up in my diction- ary," she said, as she pulled a small paperback edition from her purse. "Here it is, *sobresalto*. Has Teresa had a *sobre- salto*?"

With eyes lowered sadly, Mrs. Garcia nodded slowly. "Her mother left her."

"Her mother left her!" Heather translated, astonishment showing in her voice. Wanda cautioned her to silence as the grandmother explained the painful circumstances.

"Teresa was a 'love child', born to my daughter when she was only *17*. Last summer my daughter fell in love with a man who came to work the fields. When he left in the fall, she was heartbroken. Later he sent her money and asked her to marry him but telling her to travel there alone. He did not want to rear another man's child.

"It seemed to her the only chance for happiness. So even though it pained her greatly, she left. Teresa didn't cry for her. She just sat day after day, huddled in the corner of her crib."

"Then she has improved somewhat since this happened?" Wanda asked through Heather.

"Yes, now she follows me from room to room, but she still will not talk. She won't play with Rosita's boys."

"Time is necessary," Wanda said softly. "Even for a child."

"Next September she starts kindergarten with my boys," Rosita explained. "They'll have trouble enough adjusting to an English-speaking school. I only hope she is better by then."

"What school will they go to?" Heather asked.

"Lincoln Elementary."

"My twins go to that school," Heather exclaimed, but then her enthusiasm died as she realized how very difficult it was going to be for them. "I teach a class of 4-year-olds in Sunday school. Do you think the children would enjoy visiting my class? Perhaps it would help prepare them for kindergarten."

"I don't know," Rosita answered negatively. "They would feel out of place."

"And Teresa is not ready, I'm sure," Elena added.

"It was just an idea," Heather murmured. She noticed Wanda glance at her watch. They walked back to the Garcia living room, where Teresa was still playing with the wooden game. Wanda bent down and picked up the blocks, but when she reached for the yellow board, Teresa pulled it back and held it closely.

"Teresa, you must return that to the lady," her grandmother insisted as she took the prized yellow object and returned it to Wanda.

"It could be replaced very easily," Wanda offered. She was still squatting at Teresa's eye level when she held out the board to the child and said, "For Teresa."

The big, black eyes testified to the battle raging in the child's mind. She wanted the game so very much, but she wasn't sure she should trust the strange woman who was offering it to her.

Wanda smiled encouragingly. Teresa took two hesitant steps towards her. "For Teresa," Wanda repeated. Two small hands reached out and took hold of the board. As she stood so close, Teresa looked deep into Wanda's eyes. A perplexed look crossed the child's face. Then, to everyone's astonishment, she leaned over and kissed Wanda's cheek.

"Oh, you doll!" was all Wanda managed to say, as she fought to maintain her professional composure despite the emotion that overwhelmed her.

In the Novaks' car driving back to the Home, Wanda admitted, "I must be softening, Heather. I think I could really love that child. I can't explain it, but I find her very appealing."

"Of course you do! And that just proves you could love a child that isn't your own. I see no reason why you couldn't marry and adopt children. That's been bothering me ever since you confided your family history."

"I've been wondering how long it was going to take you to decide this." Wanda sighed. "And I realize that, when a happily married woman starts matchmaking, it is a sign of affection. I appreciate that, Heather, but I'm really not ready to start looking for a husband."

"Well, maybe not right now, but—"

"But I don't know if I will ever be ready to marry. And did you ever consider that perhaps the Lord would prefer I stay single? He did. Marriage and a family aren't the automatic solutions to every woman's reason for existence, you know."

"All right," Heather conceded. "Don't get so defensive. I wasn't trying to plan your life for you."

"I know. I'm sorry if I overreact to such suggestions. But if you only knew all the embarrassing situations I've gotten into because of someone's good intentions, you'd understand. If I get invited to one more dinner party where I'm matched up with someone's bachelor cousin or something, I think I'll scream."

"I'll bet you have had it!" Heather laughed.

"I have!" Wanda responded seriously. "Right now I'm working on writing letters to the relatives I've neglected for so long. I'm finding it emotionally draining. I'm not ready for even considering any romantic entanglements."

"I understand," Heather agreed as she turned into the driveway of the Home. "And I certainly do appreciate you taking time to visit Teresa with me."

"Oh, that was my pleasure," Wanda responded heartily. "I mean that was really a pleasure."

Chapter 13

When Don got home that evening, he gave Heather an affectionate kiss and waited for her usual question about his day.

"Don, you will never guess what I did today. I went to visit Teresa. Remember? She's the little girl Josh told the group about last week. Well, I got to know her grandmother, Elena Garcia, and a neighbor, Rosita Gile.

"And I was so worried about my limited Spanish, but you know, they are so friendly that it didn't seem to matter at all. Come to think of it, they got a kick out of me correcting myself all the time. And they have promised to help me learn to speak better. Mrs. Garcia is going to teach me some of her recipes because, when I came back after lunch, the house just smelled so good that—"

"Whoa!" Don laughed. "You are getting ahead of yourself, my breathless one. I'm glad you had such a fulfilling day, but how about starting from the beginning and giving me some of the details?"

While Don ate a hearty meal, Heather toyed with her food. She was much more interested in relating the experiences of the day than she was in eating. "Just one thing really upsets me," she concluded as Don got up to serve the coffee.

"What's that, honey?"

"Those kids. They are sharp, intelligent youngsters, but putting them into school with kids like ours who have had every advantage just doesn't seem fair. What if the situation were reversed and our boys had started out in a Spanish-speaking school? They wouldn't have seemed brilliant by any means.

"And think of all the stories, fables, and nursery rhymes most kids know before kindergarten. These Spanish-speaking children won't have an opportunity to learn them. Not knowing something that everyone else seems to know makes you feel dumb. I know, I feel that way a lot of times."

"But you don't really think you are dumb, do you?"

"No, because I have enough self-confidence to ask questions when I don't understand something. Then when I've been clued in, my self-esteem returns. But that's what worries me about those kids. What's going to happen to their self-esteem when they are placed in a school system that is not geared to most of their needs?"

"I see what you mean," Don replied thoughtfully. "Beginning their education with a feeling of inadequacy could be a handicap they might never overcome. What are you planning on doing about it?"

"Me!" Heather said in amazement. "Well, I don't know."

Don's challenge haunted her through the rest of the evening. Long after the lights had been turned out, she lay awake thinking. Finally an idea occurred to her.

"Oh, it's perfect!" she exclaimed aloud. "Everything fits together so beautifully!"

"Uh. What—how's that?" Don asked sleepily.

"Four-year-olds, those beautiful little Spanish-speaking pre-kindergarteners are 4-year-olds. That's my thing. Teaching that very age group. These kids might feel out of place with my Sunday morning class, but I know of no reason I couldn't teach a special class during the week!

"We have that gorgeous new children's building with all that equipment. It is used only one day a week! Weekday

136

classes would multiply the returns from the investment the church has made in educational space. We could fulfill a real need in the community and perhaps reach some families that we are having no contact with now.

"And it would be the perfect setup for teaching English. We have the small-size kitchen—dishes, pots, pans, nature-study stuff, books, toys, just everything needed to teach them the words they'll use in kindergarten. And I could use my puppets—I'll have to make a new one that speaks only Spanish. Then I could have the other puppets teaching him English. The kids would learn by watching. And I could let the class teach some Spanish to the puppets, but of course they wouldn't be as smart as the class ,which would make the class feel—"

"Boy, when you get an idea, you really get enthusiastic," Don interrupted.

"But don't you see what a natural this is? I'll bet Wanda would help me set up the curriculum. And what's-her-name from church, the lady who teaches kindergarten in Barrington—Sheila will know her name—I'll get her to outline what a child should know before he or she starts kindergarten. And Elena and Rosita will have some good suggestions to offer, I'm sure."

"Don't you think you should talk to the pastor about this?"

"Oh sure, I will. But I want to get my ideas thought out and on paper first so I won't sound so scatterbrained. I'll work on that tomorrow and then see him Thursday. Maybe I could start next week! Doesn't that sound exciting?"

"Yeah, but that soon?"

"I don't know why not. It would only be a few hours a day. I won't neglect you or the boys. Only four more months of school? If I plan to have them ready to enroll by September, I'll have to get with it."

"How many children are you planning on?"

"Oh, I could deal with half a dozen by myself. For any more than that, I'd need some helpers. Six would be a good number for now; then next year, after I've had some experience—"

"I hope you realize that a thing like this could snowball. You might really be letting yourself in for something."

"Well, I'll worry about that later. Right now I'm primarily concerned with three very special children. If there are two or three others who live nearby who would benefit from the classes, we'll include them. I'm so excited I don't think I'll ever get to sleep. I have so many ideas milling around in my head."

"Well, how about saving them until you have your 'logical presentation' all worked out so I can get some sleep?"

"All right, spoilsport! But something is going to come of this idea, just you wait and see."

"I believe it, sweetheart. I have great confidence in you. Why, you'll have those preschoolers so charmed that they'll learn without realizing it."

"Oh, I just thought of something," Heather confided seriously.

"What's that?"

"Well, motivation, I guess you'd call it. When we visited 'Little Appalachia,' I wanted to help those people, but out of pity, I'm afraid. Then when I thought of volunteering at the Home, that was out of a sense of duty. But these kids! Oh, Don, working with them will be a pure act of love. I'd really just love to help them."

"That's beautiful, sweetheart," Don murmured, reaching for her in the darkness and pulling her close. "And so are you."

The next morning Heather popped out of bed bright and early and full of energy. She even made the bed before she went to call the boys.

"Hey, I hope this 'Magnificent Obsession' of yours isn't going to run you ragged," Don cautioned.

"Oh, no, but I do have to keep up with my house. I'll just have to work out my schedule more efficiently so I can teach a few hours a day and still maintain my standards at home."

"You just might get to the point where you have to reexamine some of your priorities," Don warned.

"Don't worry," she called lightly as she dashed out of the room.

While her family was eating breakfast, Heather was writing a list on one of Don's yellow pads.

"What's that all about?" he asked.

"A list of calls I have to make," she replied absently. "Maybe you can think of something I've forgotten. I have Sheila, to make an appointment to talk to Dr. Wilkes tomorrow; Jan, I want her to pick up whatever books she thinks might be helpful—she'll probably have some good ideas, too; Wanda, I especially want some tips on working with Teresa; the kindergarten teacher, I'd like to make an appointment with her this weekend; and I'm going over to talk with Elena and Rosita. Any suggestions?"

"Not offhand. Don't the Garcias have a phone?"

"I don't know, but I'd have to go over there anyway. No way could I communicate by phone. Without my hands and a good deal of pantomime, we couldn't have a conversation at all," she explained with a frank, open expression.

"I believe it!" Don laughed. "You're so expressive, you don't really need words at all."

"Yeah, Mom, you really do make lots of faces," Timmy teased.

"Sure do," Tommy agreed. "But what's this all about?"

"Before long your mother is going to have the whole family taking Spanish lessons," Don teased. "When she gets enthusiastic, everyone gets sucked along in tidal-wave fashion. I'll explain it on the way to school. It's about that time."

The twins were excited about the idea of learning Spanish. As they left the house, both of them were bubbling over with so many questions that Don was sure they had inherited their mother's curiosity.

"An appointment for tomorrow?" Sheila sounded very suspicious as she repeated Heather's request. "How about 2 o'clock?"

"That will be fine. Thanks, Sheila."

"Uh, anything I could help with?"

"Not now; thanks anyway. See ya." Heather hung up before the inquisition had time to begin in earnest. An amused look crossed her face as she realized everyone who attended the midweek prayer service that evening would probably hear veiled innuendos that the Novaks were having marital difficulties. She hadn't really meant to be mysterious, but she wasn't ready yet to publicize her intentions. Telling Sheila any bit of news was tantamount to running spot announcements on TV.

Next she made a call to Jan at the library. "That sounds great!" Jan gushed, "Say, would you like me to bring the books over tonight? I could come over after the church service. We could flip through the material and perhaps come up with some good ideas."

"I'd really appreciate that, Jan. You could help me organize my thoughts before I present them to Dr. Wilkes tomorrow. I'll see you then."

Wanda's reception of her idea was even more encouraging. "I think you've come up with the perfect outlet for your talents, Heather. Those boys really responded to you. I bet Teresa will also. Would you like me to be there tonight, too?"

"I certainly would! You don't know how much your enthusiasm encourages me."

"That'll be fine. One more suggestion: why not invite Jackie? She might have some good ideas about dealing with minority groups."

"Excellent," Heather proclaimed with a snap of her fingers. "She's the one who pointed out some of the negative features in a few of the books we were using in Sunday school. Stuff like *Little Black Sambo*. She even took time to go through all our literature. I'll give her a call."

After Jackie accepted the invitation, Heather felt very pleased with the enthusiasm that was snowballing. Then she realized she'd forgotten to ask Sheila the kindergarten teacher's name. Hesitant to call back and build up the church secretary's curiosity any further, she decided to wait until she was in the office.

Climbing the wooden steps of the frame bungalow that afternoon, Heather hoped she wasn't wearing out her welcome. The broad smile that crossed Elena's face when she opened the door dispelled that worry.

As she explained the plans for the prekindergarten classes, Heather wished she had better command of the subjunctive case. She tried to make it clear that these were tentative ideas and that they would only be implemented if they approved. The two friends looked at each other blankly at first; then, as they realized just what Heather meant, they both began chattering at once. Elena gave her a big *abrazo* and exclaimed, "Thanks to God!"

Her boys were jumping up and down as Rosita gave Heather another hug which expressed not only affection but approval and gratitude. Heather would have been overwhelmed by her new friends' reactions, but the boys didn't give her a chance.

"Will you play games with us? Will you tell us stories?

When? When do we start?" they both demanded at once.

Heather glanced over at the doorway, where she thought she caught the flicker of a smile on a shy little face.

"Calm yourselves. Calm yourselves," Rosita commanded. "Give Heather a chance to talk!"

"We hope to start next week," she explained. "If so, we could take three more students, if you know of any other children who would benefit from the classes."

"Ah, certainly," Rosita exclaimed. "My husband's cousin lives near here. She has twin girls who will soon be 5. They start school next year but not here. They live across some border line, so they cannot attend Lincoln Elementary. Could they be here anyway?"

"As long as they live nearby, it shouldn't make any difference. One of the problems I must work out is transportation. I can fit six children in my station wagon easily, but, if I can get someone to pick them up in the mornings, that would give me time to set up whatever equipment I'm going to use that day. Do you have their address?"

"No, I could get there, but I don't know the names of the streets. Tonight my husband will go and tell her; then we will find a telephone and call you. All right?" she asked over the noise of the boys who never had calmed down.

"That will be fine. Then on Friday I'll go by and visit her so she won't believe she is sending her children off with a stranger. By then I should also be more definite about what times to pick them up and bring them back. So I'll see you Friday too."

As she was driving home, Heather could hardly believe how light and happy she felt. She had never experienced such a sense of exhilaration and purpose. The planning meeting would not convene for several long hours. How could she contain her joy that long? She'd just have to call Don and share it with him.

Shortly after the church service that evening, the chattering women were encamped in the Novak den. The *clickety-clack* of a typewriter punctuated the hum of activity. Don settled down in his big black leather chair to read the paper. He understood a little better how Heather felt when his work kept them separated.

"How'd it go?" he asked after the "planners" had left and Heather finally joined him in the family room.

"Oh, just great, honey," she replied as she fairly exuded enthusiasm. "Those are some real sharp gals; they came up with some very helpful, practical suggestions. Jan is a fantastic organizer. Would you like to see what we've done tonight?"

"Not now; it's late. Maybe in the morning."

"Well, one thing we decided I think you will approve of; that's to have classes four mornings a week. That will give me Mondays to give the house a really thorough cleaning so it will be easier to keep up with chores the rest of the week. Another thing: Rosita's husband called. They have three more children lined up to attend. That gives me the six I wanted."

"Heather, I'm really glad to see you so excited about this project. You have my wholehearted approval. But do you realize that for the past two days you haven't once asked me about things that concern me? Don't you care any more how my day goes?"

"Why, Donald Novak!" she exclaimed as she walked over and sat on his lap. "I do believe you are pouting!"

"Well, I guess I am at that!" Don had to laugh at himself. "I just don't want you to get so involved in any activity that you forget I'm number one."

"I can't believe this conversation!" Heather chortled. "Do you realize we've reversed roles?"

"I guess it does sound that way. *Hmmmm*," Don pondered, "have I really been a 'male chauvinist pig'?"

"Well, maybe just a piglet," Heather teased, as she snuggled up closer and began chewing on his ear.

Don gave her a warm, loving kiss and then whispered in her ear, "You are the most continually fascinating female I have ever known."

Heather drew back and thought about that a moment and then replied, "I think that's the nicest compliment I've ever been given."

Heather felt quite professional the next afternoon as she gathered up the neatly typed outlines and placed them in a file folder. Swinging the strap of her oversized purse onto her shoulder, she started toward the hall closet to get her coat. To her great delight, the full-length hall mirror revealed that her cranberry-red pantsuit no longer was pulled taut across her bottom. All the extra activity in the past week hadn't given her the opportunity to do much nibbling; that fact showed!

"The pastor hasn't returned from lunch yet," Sheila explained as she tucked a couple of strands of her brassy-colored hair behind her ears. "He should be here in just a minute."

"Fine," Heather replied. "I need the name and number of our church member who teaches kindergarten. You know who I mean; she's a tall, thin woman with black hair. She usually sits on the right side of the auditorium."

"Oh, of course, Mrs. Eiklekraut. Everyone has trouble with her name." Sheila pulled open a cabinet containing the membership list, wrote the name, number, and address on a three-by-five-inch card, and handed it to Heather. "Has this anything to do with the experiment?" she asked casually.

"The experiment?" Heather repeated.

"You didn't think it was still a secret, did you?" Sheila questioned as she put on a phony, wide-mouthed smile. "Why the whole church is abuzz with the news that part of The Group has embarked on some mysterious adventure. When you have a special meeting with only a select few invited, people naturally get curious. I'll bet tonight will be the largest gathering ever. You will have an explanation, won't you?"

"I imagine it will be discussed," Heather replied. She was relieved to hear the pastor's footsteps moving down the hall.

"Well, I'll see you tonight," Sheila announced significantly.

"I am so very sorry to be late, Heather," Dr. Wilkes apologized profusely. "I had a luncheon meeting that just dragged on and on."

"Oh, that's all right," Heather replied as she glanced at her watch. "It's only a few minutes."

"Well, walk right into my office. I'll give you my undivided attention," he promised nervously. "Here, take this chair next to my desk; it's quite comfortable."

Heather sat down and watched as the pastor adjusted the venetian blinds so that they would admit light without shining directly into her eyes. He then crossed the book-lined room and positioned the door so that it was open a few inches. This action puzzled Heather at first; then it amused her as she realized he was protecting their reputations by not being alone with her in a closed room as he perched on the edge of his chair behind the immaculate desk.

"Well, really it's something I'd like to do," Heather explained, "but I'll need permission to use my Sunday-school classroom four mornings a week. I'm planning on . . .." And she was off and running. The pastor listened silently as she explained the need she had discovered in their community and how she hoped to alleviate the problem. She pulled copies of her plans from the folder. The pastor lined them up symmetrically on his desk and glanced over them as she continued her monologue.

"So you see, there would be no financial outlay by the church," she concluded. "I'd be personally responsible for any damages, should they occur. I'd clean the room myself."

Dr. Wilkes leaned back in his armchair and tapped a bony forefinger pensively against his thin lips. "I'm very encouraged to see you so enthusiastic about serving others, Heather," he stated at last. "I'm sure we can find some worthwhile outlet for your energies within the framework of our church functions, but I sincerely doubt the wisdom of beginning a project such as you have outlined."

"But why?" Heather exploded. "This seems like a perfect means of extending our church's outreach!"

"For one thing, our children's building was dedicated to religious instruction. What you propose would be going far afield from that."

"But I'd tell them Bible stories. I couldn't preach to them or teach them doctrine, but they are too young for that anyway.

"Also, these children are not part of our church family," he continued as he ignored her comments. "I sincerely doubt that the elders would approve using our facilities for outsiders. Then, too, we have insurance to consider. I'm certain our present policy would not cover such usage of our buildings."

"In other words, you don't want those dirty little Mexican kids messing up our precious new edifice!"

"Why, Heather!" he remonstrated softly. "I made no such inference. I'm certain they would be welcomed to any of our regular services."

"But they couldn't understand them!"

"Well, if you feel so strongly about this, I could appoint a committee to investigate the matter. These things take time; but, if they feel our church has an obligation to provide this type of instruction, their recommendation would be considered by our board of elders. Then if the elders agreed, they would present a proposal to the church that we establish classes such as you have suggested. If the church as a whole—"

"And if all those *if's* are resolved, it would take at least a year! That would be too late for these children who need help now. Why can't I just use that one room for 12 hours a week? If any objections arise, can we not deal with them then?"

"I couldn't authorize anything like that. Don't you realize we have certain procedures that must be followed?"

"And you are afraid you'd be climbing out on a limb if you bypassed any of them?"

"Now, don't turn this into my personal responsibility, Heather. I didn't establish the rules. By what authority do you think I could break them?"

"Dr. Wilkes," Heather demanded vehemently, "what do you think Jesus would do in this situation?"

The pastor blinked, hesitated, then rose from his chair and walked to the window. Tipping one of the slats in the blind, he stared thoughtfully into the cold winter sky. As Heather watched the emotions that were displayed on his thin, pensive face, she realized the battle that was raging within him. She regretted having spoken so accusingly.

With a deep sigh, the gray-haired minister turned from the window. Settling back down in his chair, he clasped his hands together on the desk before him and stoically proclaimed, "Heather, if Jesus were pastor of this church, He would be hamstrung by the same rules, regulations, and traditions that I am."

"Then I'll find a church that is willing to do something!" she declared.

"By all means, try, but I sincerely doubt that you'll find one near here," he replied.

Unable to trust herself to make any further comments, Heather jammed her papers back into the folder and stalked from the room.

"Well, I hope you got an earful!" she snapped sarcastically at the open-mouthed secretary, as she picked up her coat and stormed out of the office.

As she raced to the church parking lot, she climbed into her car without even taking time to put on her coat. She was too infuriated to be cold anyway. The realization that she was shaking so hard that she could hardly get the key into the ignition made her even more angry. Driving home safely took every bit of concentration she could muster.

"I have never been so absolutely livid in my life," she realized, as she drew water to make a pot of tea. "I need to talk to someone. No, first I need to get control of myself," she decided when she spilled water all over the floor on the way to the stove.

Grabbing some paper towels, she started wiping the floor. Bitter tears began to flow. "Lord, how could this happen?" she demanded from her kneeling position in the middle of her kitchen floor. "This whole idea seemed so clearly to be from You. Yet, if it were Your will, how could it be stymied like this?"

"I—I feel so totally wiped out," she confessed. "I've heard people talk about 'mountaintops of joy' and 'valleys of deep despair'. I've always thought they were exaggerating—that such swings of emotion were reserved for manic depressives. But, Lord, that's just how I feel—as if I'd been knocked off some high escarpment into a deep pit.

"How can I face our friends tonight? The rest of The Group, especially, will laugh and say our whole experiment is ridiculous.

"But even worse," she choked, "how will I ever explain to those precious children that they are not wanted?"

Chapter 14

Don held open the car door as Heather slid in and then walked around to the driver's seat. "OK," he said over the sound of the engine igniting, "want to tell me about it now that the twins can't overhear?"

"I guess so," Heather replied rather reluctantly. "It was a bad scene, Don. Really bad. I'm not only disappointed at not receiving the permission I expected but also embarrassed at how very poorly I dealt with the situation.

"I had built myself up for a fall with visions of waltzing into the pastor's office, laying my fantastic plans before him, and having him overwhelmed with my great self-sacrificing, magnanimous dedication. I was all prepared to answer, 'Think nothing of it, Pastor; I'm sure I will enjoy working with those children. Besides, it's what I believe Jesus would do in my place!'

"Yeck, how pietistic can you get," Heather berated herself. "And then, when he not only was not impressed but disapproved the idea, I lashed out at him like a lioness protecting her cubs! I accused him of being prejudiced and uncaring. I was really vicious."

"I can just envision it," Don replied, as he turned a corner into a narrow country lane. "My spunky wife breathing fire and brimstone and ready to lead an assault on the foes of justice."

"Don't sound so amused! It wasn't funny. I will have to apologize to him. I'm sure he isn't prejudiced personally. He gave some logical-sounding reasons, but it boils down to his belief that some of our church members wouldn't want those 'foreigners' in our building; he seems very reluctant to displease anyone. What's the expression? He doesn't want to rock the boat?"

"Yeah, he doesn't want to rock the boat, so you got the wind knocked out of your sails."

"I sure did," she admitted. "And now I'm dreading telling my enthusiastic cohorts the bad news. Sure hope I can get them aside so the whole group doesn't have to get in on this."

"Wow, look at the cars!" Don exclaimed, as they neared the Lindholms' modernistic manor.

"Sheila warned me there was a lot of curiosity about our experiment. Good thing we're meeting here. Not many homes would accommodate this size crowd."

The Novaks were ushered into the huge, high-ceilinged combination living and dining room. Every seat was filled. Sheila Graham was wedged into the Danish modern couch next to her husband, Bob, where she had a commanding view of The Group. Jan and Wanda scooted apart, making space for Heather to sit with them on the raised marble hearth. Don dropped down to the thickly carpeted floor next to Josh.

"You'd almost think this was prearranged," Jan whispered to Heather.

"What do you mean?"

"Look around. Everybody involved in the experiment is seated right in the middle of the crowd."

Heather acknowledged the correctness of Jan's observations as Bill Lindholm rose to call the meeting to order. He pushed the few remaining strands of his hair into place and began rocking his huge body back and forth on his heels.

"We're very honored to host what must be the largest turnout The Group has ever had. Welcome! I only hope we can maintain our usual informality despite the size of the crowd. First off, I understand congratulations are in order. Kenny, would you like to give us an up-to-the-minute report?"

Kenny beamed at all the well-wishers. "They're both doing fine," he announced proudly. "This afternoon I walked Sally Ann down to the nursery to see our son for the first time. He's a scrawny little critter and bears a close resemblance to a skinned rabbit, but we shore are mighty pleased with him and extremely happy that he's OK.

"I reckon you all heard what a close call they both had. I want to thank all of you who prayed for them, especially the friends who took time to be with us in the hospital when things were lookin' gloomy. I could never express how much that meant."

"We're all very happy for you," Bill spoke for the group. "And since you've got the floor, Kenny, why don't you fill us in on what happened at the last meeting."

"Be glad to," Kenny began in his slow drawl. "That snow-storm gyped some of you out of quite an experience. You see, I had just read the book *In His Steps* and was wondering whether in our modern society people could make all decisions as Jesus would. We knocked that question around quite a bit."

"And what did you conclude?" one of the newcomers, Judge Newcomb, asked.

"After our brainstorming, we arrived at a great conclusion," Al explained, "that we didn't know." After the laughter and good-natured chides died down, he continued. "But we agreed to try it for one week. When we got together last Thursday, we found we'd learned a lot."

"Well, Josh and I realized that giving money is no substitute for personal involvement," Jackie volunteered with a smile that seemed to draw her audience together.

"That's right," Josh agreed. "I was writing out some

152

checks one night. I tried to imagine Jesus sitting at my desk. Mailing a check so some unknown black student could receive a scholarship suddenly became a cold, sterile act. Jesus' whole life centered around people. Even though sending the money was a good thing, it seemed clear it wasn't enough. We had to have a deeper commitment to individuals.

"After a good deal of discussion, Jackie and I decided we could serve our people and the community at the same time by helping some of the blacks who worked nearby to find housing in the suburbs. We've met a lot of opposition, but we're determined to keep trying."

"But how can anyone stop you?" Heather demanded. "Isn't it illegal to refuse—?"

"Oh, Heather, you live such a sheltered life!" Jackie laughed. "You'd be surprised at all the ingenious ways there are of closing doors."

"It looks like the only way we'll be able to pull it off is to become landlords ourselves," Josh explained. "We're financially solvent and have lived and worked in the community too long to be refused credit. We're considering some rental property just down the block from our home. If all goes as planned, our first tenants will be one of Don's employees and his family."

"Hank?" Heather asked.

Josh nodded affirmatively.

"Oh, good! They're fine folks," she exclaimed to the crowd. "How interesting that you two didn't let opposition stop you!"

"Of course not," Jackie replied indignantly. "When you know you're right, you can't take *no* as a negative. That just means you must try another way."

"We haven't even gotten a *no* yet," Jan commented. "No response at all."

"Guess I'd better explain that," Al added. "I've asked my boss if ISC would be willing to give me a year's leave of absence to devote to the Bible Translators. I believe I can set up a computer system that would help speed their work along."

A murmur of disbelief spread around through the periphery of The Group.

"Well, even if nothing springs from the idea, I think Al has traveled a long way by being willing to leave his precious computer at ISC," Jan defended her spouse to the disbelievers. "Making this decision wasn't easy!"

"Everyone realized that, Jan," the genial Bill Lindholm explained. "We're quite flabbergasted." He looked around at the crowd and sensed he was speaking for everyone before he added. "And very pleased."

The bond of unity that was building within The Group encouraged Al to continue. "I just might take a cue from Josh and Jackie and take a trip to the translators' headquarters to discuss the possibilities with some of their leaders. But right now I think my wife should share her big news."

All eyes turned expectantly to Jan. "Well, this philosophy of being more 'people-related' that evolved from trying to react as Jesus would has even affected my writing. I am thrilled to announce that I've sold my first article to a major magazine!"

Calls of congratulations were heard from all around. Heather gave Jan a happy hug. "In today's mail I received an acceptance from *Woman's World*," Jan explained to her number-one encourager. Heather beamed back with an almost maternal pride.

"This experiment sounds more interesting all the time," the silver-haired judge commented. "Kenny, how has it affected you?"

"Well, I've decided to take fewer speaking engagements so that Sally Ann and I can help some of the folks who have moved from back in the hills and adjust to city livin'. As long as I'm in baseball, that will probably be our field of service. "But, ya know, Your Honor, one of the things we've all discovered is that this decidin' like Jesus would kinda gets to ya. It isn't a thing you can do for just one week. Your attitudes and ambitions start changing. Before you know it, your whole future looks different. I s'pose some of you will think this idea is amusing, but I've been seriously considering that, when my playing days are over, I just might move back to the hills and get into politics like good ole Vinegar Ben Mizell did."

The Group did seem surprised, but no one laughed.

"I jest keep wondering why these folks are forced to leave their hones and kin," Kenny continued. "Why can't something be done to create more jobs back in the hills so they don't have to uproot their families and move to the big cities that seem so hostile to them? If I could get enough folks to vote for me, I'd sure work hard to help them."

"Oh—oh, Kenny's going modest on us again," Jackie teased. "Why, I bet he's the biggest hero to ever emerge from those hills. I fully expect to hear one day that he's been elected governor."

"That's a very commendable ambition," the judge commented. "Our country could use more Christians in places of leadership. I don't see why anyone would find your idea amusing."

"It's pure prejudice," Don quipped. "Politicians and sales people are always being joked about, but there are honest and dishonest members of every occupation."

"Right, it's just tougher to find an honest salesman," Bob Graham teased with a deep boisterous guffaw.

"Well, I'm going to do what I can to change that reputation," Don declared. "And so are my sales people, whether they want to or not. I've decided Jesus would supervise His employees closer than I have been doing. I want all my customers to be treated as fairly as my friends are."

"And how did your employees react to that declaration?" Bob asked.

"Oh, they all agree that I'll probably go bankrupt," Don replied lightly. "I'll be interested to see if they're right."

"I've been wondering," Sheila Graham interjected in her most mellow, saccharin tone, "weren't you at that meeting of The Group, Wanda?"

The Group responded to Sheila's pointed question as if she had cracked a whip. A tense silence fell on the motionless crowd. Wanda felt Heather stiffen beside her, but she placed a restraining hand on her arm before her friend could rush to her defense.

"Yes, I was," Wanda responded. She was very aware of everyone's curiosity. "And asking what Jesus would do if He were living my life has made me rethink my lifestyle. One decision I had to make was to stop being such a 'lady of mystery,'" she quoted as she looked directly at Sheila. The Group all knew the loose-tongued church secretary well enough to realize the source of the quote. Sheila squirmed uncomfortably and shot an accusing glance at Heather, who merely smiled frankly.

"I'm afraid I haven't been as friendly as I should have been," Wanda continued, "but these past two weeks have pulled down some of the barriers I had build around me. One of the most meaningful experiences was an impromptu prayer meeting we had in Sally Ann's hospital room last Saturday. It was a beautiful experience. We had among us a feeling of intimacy that I hadn't allowed myself to have for many years. I'm sure the others felt it, too."

"Yeah, we sure did!" Jan exclaimed. "Al and I have talked about it a great deal. We had such an overpowering awareness of love, both for the Lord and for each other."

"It was really unique," Al chimed in. He hoped to explain the experience to those who had missed it. "This 'oneness' with Christ brings you to a special relationship with others who are similarly aligned."

"Exactly!" Josh agreed. "I've heard brotherhood preached all my life, but I never really understood the full implication of the term until we were standing there, hands joined in that circle."

"This is just what Sally Ann and I felt!" Kenny exclaimed. "But we thought it was just us, since it was our baby we were praying for. I'm glad to know you all shared the same emotions."

"We did," Heather assured him. "It was a very special experience."

"And especially meaningful to me," Wanda continued. "It convinced me that I need people. If you will all forgive me for being so cold and impersonal, I hope to change. I've been such a private person for so long that changing will take time, so please have patience with me.

"Now, Heather, why don't you tell them about your plans?"

"Oh, yes, do!" Jan agreed.

Heather felt herself flush as the spotlight of attention was turned in her direction. "I've become involved with some very special 4-year-olds," she explained. "These children live near here and will be attending local schools next year, but they don't speak English. I've decided to provide classes geared to preparing them for kindergarten."

Don raised his eyebrows quizzically while a murmur of interest swept through the crowd. Sheila leaned forward intently and wondered what form of rebellion Heather was planning.

"These classes will be meeting four mornings a week," Heather declared determinedly, "in our home."

"What?" Sheila gasped. "You're going to take those dirty little, uh, those farm children into your beautiful house?"

"They are not dirty!" Heather almost shouted. "I've been in their homes. They are every bit as clean as mine. Even if they weren't, children are more important than dirt!"

"But—but, those immigrant children will tear your house apart!"

"I'm an immigrant child," Don snapped, with anger flushing his normally calm exterior. "My parents migrated from Poland shortly before I was born."

"Oh, but that's different," Sheila maintained.

"How is it different?" Jackie demanded, her black eyes flashing. "Because it doesn't show?"

"Well, at least he speaks English!"

"I spoke Polish first!"

"But—but," Sheila stuttered as she swiveled her head around and searched for someone who would agree with her. She met only stony silence. Jackie opened her mouth to continue the argument, but with a shake of his head Josh restrained her.

"Being the child of immigrant parents has never been a handicap to me," Don continued more calmly, "and I don't think it should be for any child."

"When you stop and analyze it," Wanda commented, "prejudice is very illogical."

"Oh, course it is," Heather agreed. "And I've been . . .." She hesitated as her eyes found Don's. "I've been re-evaluating my priorities. I have decided the time and devotion I lavish on my house would be much better invested in those beautiful children. I hope my husband agrees."

The slow, special grin that Heather valued so highly spread across Don's face. She felt the caress of his eyes as keenly as a physical touch.

"I've never been more proud of you," Don croaked hoarsely.

"I believe I must add one thing to this discussion," Heather continued. "If any of you is contemplating making this decision for your own lives, I must warn you that I've discovered promising the Lord something is a dangerous thing. He just might call you on it. When I promised I'd willingly use my home for Him, I was thinking of an occasional evening meeting of adults." She smiled. "And look what I've gotten myself into! But I love it."

"Well, *In His Steps* appears to have been quite a success," the judge decreed.

"No, not really," Al disagreed. "Sheldon thought his book was going to change the course of world history, but it obviously hasn't."

"But can it really be considered a failure?" Heather asked. "It might not have changed world history, but it has certainly changed our lives, hasn't it?"

CPSIA information can be obtained at www.ICGtesting.com
228017LV00007B/160/P